SHARING THE FAITH THAT YOU LOVE

Four Simple Ways to Be Part of the New Evangelization

John and Therese Boucher

the WORD among us® press

Published by The Word Among Us Press
7115 Guilford Road
Frederick, Maryland 21704
www.wau.org

18 17 16 15 14   1 2 3 4 5

ISBN: 978-1-59325-251-9
eISBN: 978-1-59325-455-1

Nihil Obstat: Rev. Michael Morgan

Censor Librorum

December 12, 2013

Imprimatur: +Most Rev. Felipe J. Estévez,

Bishop of St. Augustine

December 12, 2013

Cover design by Koechel Peterson & Associates

Made and printed in the United States of America

Library of Congress Control Number: 2013948980

Dedicated to

Robert Fenner

who taught us how to share faith with love

1954–2012

and

Dr. Wayne G. Rollins

filled with zeal for the gospel.

Contents

Foreword

How I wish John and Therese Boucher's book, *Sharing the Faith That You Love,* had been available years ago when I first started helping Catholics evangelize!

Coming from an openly anti-Catholic, fundamentalist background, I had breezily presumed that most Catholics were not real "believers" but baptized pagans who were all busy "earning" their salvation. After I became Catholic, I heard an older woman talk in tones of the greatest love and reverence about receiving the Lord Jesus in the Eucharist, and I was instantly convicted of my arrogance, and repented as a result.

After that, I told myself that the mysterious Catholic silence about conversion and evangelism that I kept encountering must be the result of a spiritual reality that I, who had been raised in the extroverted world of American evangelicals, could not easily understand or appreciate. I told myself that Catholic culture is introverted, and that introverted people do not talk easily or casually about such deep matters. Catholics are *silent* because they are *deep*, living out of a relationship with God that transcends words.

For eighteen years, I held onto this diagnosis while simultaneously struggling to grasp the spiritual poverty I often encountered when I asked Catholics to tell me about their experiences of being used by God. I assumed that some lingering Protestant ways of thinking were hampering my ability to hit "pay dirt." I must be asking the wrong questions or using the wrong language, I thought, to evoke the sharing of the spiritual depth that I was certain had to be there.

Of all the unlikely remedies, it was a dyed-in-the-wool cradle Catholic who finally set me straight. Fr. Mike Fones, OP, my second co-director at the Catherine of Siena Institute, is a lifelong believing and practicing Catholic, along with his parents and siblings. Fr. Mike never took a "vacation" from being Catholic or spent any time in the Protestant world. To top it all of—the ultimate Catholic success story—he become a priest!

After a discouraging experience of listening to small group discussions at an early Making Disciples seminar, our teaching team was eating lunch and discussing why the participants found it so difficult to identify spiritually hungry people in their parishes. I was still blaming myself because I had written the exercise when Fr. Mike turned to me and said, "Sherry, give it up. It isn't because you were once Protestant or aren't asking the right questions. You aren't finding it because it is not there. Most Catholics are silent about conversion and a relationship with Christ because most of us have nothing to say."

Or, as I would put it now, lay Catholics haven't been reading the Bible or the *Catechism* or papal encyclicals to find out what it means to be Catholic; *they have been reading each other*. The fact that ordinary lay Catholics don't *talk* about intentional discipleship makes it very, very difficult for most of them to *think* about it. A powerful "culture of silence" around conversion and discipleship is the primary reason why so many active Catholic adults and leaders have told me, "I did not know I could have a personal relationship with God until today."

The Bouchers not only understand all this, but they have created a terrific way to break the silence! *Sharing the Faith That You Love* is intended for use by individuals or small groups who are interested in exploring evangelization. This book is the field-tested fruit of the Bouchers' decades of experience with real-life evangelization with family and friends, as well as the many years of teaching the art of evangelization in small groups at both parish and diocesan levels. Their book will help Catholic men and women embark upon a relationship with God for the first time, or strengthen their existing relationship, while at the same time teaching them how to help others encounter Jesus in a life-changing way in the midst of his Church.

Sharing the Faith That You Love is filled with encouraging real-life stories, powerful prayer experiences, inspiring quotes from saints and popes, creative and thought-provoking "spiritual work-outs," and exercises that will get you in touch with your own experience of God as well as with the obstacles that are keeping you from effectively sharing the faith with others. This book will help you and your fellow parishioners move beyond wordless witness.

One of the most encouraging aspects of the book is its focus on trusting the work of the Holy Spirit and taking the long view. John and Therese tell several stories of evangelical conversations that seemed to be failures at the time but, years later, were revealed to be turning points in another person's relationship with God. They gift us with a warm, balanced, evangelical Catholic wisdom at its practical best, written in language that will speak to both cradle Catholics and to converts from other backgrounds.

Every pastoral leader who is interested in helping Catholics become comfortable with an intentional relationship with Jesus and with sharing that relationship with others should encourage them to read *Sharing the Faith That You Love.*

Sherry A. Weddell
Co-Director, Catherine of Siena Institute
Author of *Forming Intentional Disciples: The Path to Knowing and Following Jesus*

INTRODUCTION

"Life is just one big disappointment after another," Therese thought as she trudged down the stairs to the campus post office. "Here I am, at my second-choice college. Here I am, with one of my horrible migraines. Here I am, a failure at pursuing a religious vocation. What's next?"

A lingering feeling of depression clung to Therese as she opened her mailbox. "A junk-mail invitation to an Antioch Weekend retreat! What good would that do?" she thought. "I've already tried novenas, rosaries, and months of Friday night benedictions."

So into the trash went the invitation. Then a student nearby found the same junk mail in her box. "I can't believe it!" she said between squeals of glee. "I'm invited, I'm invited! I've been hoping this would happen for months."

Therese looked at this ecstatic girl, then at the trash can, then back at the girl. Then she fished out that invitation and went on the retreat. It was a turning point in her faith.

Maybe you can trace your experience of a personal faith back to a significant moment or two, as Therese can. Maybe you have known only a quiet, almost invisible trickle of God's presence. Perhaps it is even a stretch to say that you love your faith right now. Whatever the case may be, God is inviting you to a deeper faith and a new spiritual compassion. And that deeper faith will bring you to the threshold of sharing your faith with others through four simple steps: praying, caring, sharing faith, and daring to invite others into a faith-filled community. God is inviting you to be a part of the New Evangelization, part of a renewed Church-wide effort to reach out to inactive, marginal Catholics and those who are unchurched with a greater awareness of the gift of faith that God offers every human person.

God's invitation to share your faith may have begun with a growing concern about your adult children or about nieces and nephews who don't go to church. Perhaps God is speaking to you through neighbors and relatives who drive by your parish to go to Sunday services elsewhere or through friends who have died without funeral prayers or burial in a Catholic cemetery. Perhaps you have been jarred by church attendance surveys with sobering statistics like these: as of 2008, only 23 percent of Catholics attended Sunday Mass each week, while head counts by officials in several dioceses in the Northeast reflect attendance levels as being closer to 15 percent.[1] Another study found that only 37 percent of Catholics know that Easter is about the resurrection of Christ,[2] while a third study notes that only 48 percent of Catholics are certain that one can have a personal relationship with God.[3]

Your own experiences and observations, as well as these statistics, are just a few of the ways God might be calling you to "wake up" and find new ways to share the faith that you are called to love. But how do you take steps to share faith when such a task seems foreign or overwhelming? How do you embrace the New Evangelization for the sake of others? The Vatican's Congregation for the Doctrine of the Faith, in a 2007 document entitled *Doctrinal Note on Some Aspects of Evangelization* and signed by Pope Benedict XVI, said, "*To evangelize* does not mean simply to teach a doctrine, but to proclaim Jesus Christ by one's words and actions, that is, to make oneself an instrument of his presence and action in the world."[4] So let's begin with a willingness to be instruments of Christ's presence and to learn more about sharing our faith with others.

Sharing Your Faith in Jesus

Through baptism you are called to embrace Jesus as the way, the truth, the life, and the purpose behind all of your actions. And through the Holy Spirit, you have been strengthened to live out this baptismal calling in simple but dynamic ways. So stop and invite the Holy Spirit to come and stir up the waters of your baptism. These living waters are not meant to stagnate. Baptism is an ongoing reality that empowers you to acknowledge Jesus in your everyday world as your Shepherd, Emmanuel, Brother, Lord, Teacher, and Redeemer, especially in ways that bring others to Jesus. Pope Benedict XVI pointed out, "The proclamation of and witness to the Gospel are the first service that Christians can render to every person and to the entire human race, called as they are to communicate to all God's love, which was fully manifested in Jesus Christ, the one Redeemer of the world."[5]

You might still be wondering, "How could I ever communicate God's loving presence or even proclaim Jesus through my actions? How could I ever bring anyone back to God or to the Church? I'm not an expert or an evangelist, and I don't want to knock on doors!" Fear not! We will help you see the details of your everyday life in the light of a lived faith. We will help you move from accidental kindnesses and invisible beliefs toward intentional acts of faith that enable others to experience Jesus in new ways.

Don't worry. You don't have to argue someone back to church, or preach on a sidewalk, or force someone to believe, or show everyone your "spiritual underwear." This book explores four simple ways that people "catch" faith from one another, whether accidentally or intentionally. This book describes evangelization as arising from a God-given spiritual compassion for loved ones and friends who don't know and love Jesus and his body, the Church. This book is also about being grounded and centered in the dynamic life of the Trinity. That dynamic life—the repeating cycle of creation, redemption, and sanctification—moves us forward in becoming a vital part of bringing the world of our everyday relationships back to the Father, with Jesus our Lord, through the power of the Holy Spirit.

Steps to Sharing Your Faith

Our goal is to help you understand ways that you already share your faith, as well as new ways to enter more deeply into the gospel cycle of praying, caring, sharing, and daring to invite others into a faith community. Our hope is to offer insights and strategies for what has been traditionally called "pre-evangelization" as well as ways to cross over into evangelization. We believe that God is constantly challenging each of us to an ongoing awareness that "in him we live and move and have our being" (Acts 17:28). We know that the Holy Spirit can nudge you with glimpses of God's presence in your life and even in the lives of those around you. We know that God can help you build upon the quiet, caring witness of everyday life and move into intentional sharing. We believe that with a little knowledge about simple faith-sharing skills, these glimpses of God's presence can empower you to reach out to empty hearts and to fill empty Sunday pews.

Sharing the Faith That You Love begins by exploring the essential gift of zeal that must come before the other steps—before prayer, caring, sharing, and daring to invite. In chapter 1, we meet Jesus, the first model of the gift of zeal, especially as he emerged from his baptism in the Jordon and his soul-searching experience in the desert with a profound zeal for sharing his Father's love. Next, in chapter 2, we focus on evangelizing prayer. We will follow Jesus, whose prayers to his Father became a wellspring for reaching out to others. Then we will explore ways to embrace evangelizing prayer. In chapter 3, we will consider the compassionate care that Jesus offered to others and our own call to caring service in the name and presence of Jesus.

Chapter 4 explores the ways we can share our faith with others, focusing on how Jesus shared about his Father, both with individuals like Nicodemus and with groups of people like the apostles. We will also consider the many simple ways to share our faith in day-to-day conversations. In chapter 5, we will examine the ways in which Jesus invited many people into the community of his followers, such as the rich young man and even his own doubting disciples. Then we will move on to exploring God's promptings to invite others into our faith community. And finally, in chapter 6, we will consider the call to evangelize that each of us shares with all the other members of our parish—the call to bring the Good News of Jesus Christ into the whole world.

How to Use This Book

This book can be used by you as an individual or in the context of a small group of people who would like to study ways to share faith with others. Each chapter offers several tools for exploring our common baptismal calling to share faith with love. The goal is to stretch your capacity for meaningful encounters with the people around you who are hungry for the Good News of Jesus. Feel free to consult the glossary of terms at the back of the book when you encounter a word or phrase that seems unfamiliar. Each chapter is divided into several sections:

Opening Prayer: Many of these prayers are from the writings of the saints, who inspire us as we respond to God's call. We suggest that you pray them aloud.

Opening Scripture: This passage sets the tone for discovering what God is saying to us.

Mini-Witness: These short stories are examples of what God can do as we embrace the mission to evangelize. They are models for appreciating what God may be doing in your own life or in the lives of others.

Part One explores God's personal invitation to faith and to a meaningful relationship with the Father, Son, and Holy Spirit. The goal is to realize your unique call to live your faith in Jesus.

Spiritual Workout: The content in Part One is followed by an exercise for growth and for assessing your thoughts about the topic. The exercise has two parts: a questionnaire with *specific instructions in italics,* and a series of reflection questions to help you explore your initial responses to Part One. Your responses to the questions can be shared with a spiritual friend or in a small group setting.

Part Two: This section offers a vision of the many ways you can be part of the New Evangelization and explores simple ways that God empowers you to reach out to others.

Spiritual Workout: As in Part One, the content is followed by an exercise to help you move forward in sharing your faith. (For an additional exercise on the same topic, see the New Evangelization Workouts section.) The questionnaire and reflection questions will help you consider ways you can implement the suggestions. Responses to these questions can also be shared.

Closing Prayer: This serves as a starting point for gathering your thoughts and getting ready to take what God has taught you into your everyday life. This prayer could be used on a daily basis until you move on to the next chapter.

New Evangelization Workouts: In addition to the two exercises included within each chapter, there is a third exercise that is appropriate for each of the chapter's themes. These are located in the New Evangelization Workouts section. It is not necessary to do the third exercise, but it is there for you as an additional resource.

All of the exercises in the book have been part of both diocesan and parish training workshops. Many have also appeared in *Evangelization Exchange*, a free online newsletter of the Paulist Evangelization Ministries.[6]

Suggestions for Faith-Sharing Groups

If you are using this book in a faith-sharing group, we suggest that the group agree on the amount of reading to be done before the session. We also recommend that you finish at least one of the Spiritual Workout sections in preparation for each meeting.

When you gather:

- Pray the Opening Prayer and Scripture passage.

- Read an excerpt from Part One aloud. (Two or three paragraphs would refresh people's minds on the topic.)

- Share the reflection questions following Part One. (Allow about fifteen to twenty minutes for discussion.)

- If time permits, do the same with Part Two.

- End with the Closing Prayer.

If the group is large, you can divide everyone into subgroups of three or four people, unless otherwise noted. Feel free to contact us for additional guidance about using this book in a group setting through www.christkey.com or through www.johnandtherese-boucher.com.

The concluding chapter in this book offers guidelines and encouragement for the times when these four simple ways of evangelizing are beyond you. Remember, in the same way that Jesus did not abandon his disciples after inviting them to "go therefore and make disciples of all nations" (Matthew 28:19), he does not leave you alone with such an important task. When your efforts to share your faith are difficult, the Holy Spirit beckons and strengthens you. The Spirit of the living God will continue to teach you how to be an evangelizing disciple of Jesus so that you can share another person's crosses and rejoice in their resurrection on the road to heaven.

John and Therese Boucher

Spiritual Workout

Here is an introductory exercise about baptismal strength and passion that will prepare you for working your way through this book.

> Therefore we have been buried with him by baptism into death, so that, just as Christ was raised from the dead by the glory of the Father, so we too might walk in newness of life. (Romans 6:4)

Jesus acted with humility and devotion to his Father. Even though he was conceived by the Holy Spirit to be without sin, he willingly submitted to baptism. He continued to seek more and more of the Spirit. Jesus chose to surrender to an ongoing anointing from the Holy Spirit, and he willingly responded to his Father's voice compelling him forward.

Can we do any less in response to the power of God's love that has been unleashed through Baptism, strengthened by Confirmation, and sustained by the Eucharist? Take a moment to look back at the beginning of your own relationship with God through the Sacrament of Baptism. Ponder the descent of the Holy Spirit upon you in the midst of your family and in the company of the whole communion of saints.

1. Where were you baptized? Do you know the date, the church, and the city? What are three things you know about your baptism? For example, who were your godparents? Were other relatives and friends in attendance? Do you have any keepsakes from your baptism? Do you know any other significant details?

2. How has the meaning of your baptism changed over the years? What kind of baptismal calling have you experienced? What strengths has God given you? What is God calling you to do with your baptism today?

3. Consider how Pope Benedict XVI's challenge might apply to you: "We cannot keep to ourselves the words of eternal life given to us in our encounter with Jesus Christ: they are meant for everyone, for every man and woman. . . . It is our responsibility to pass on what, by God's grace, we ourselves have received."[7]

Baptismal Prayer

Take me to you and give me to drink from your saving wells. Yes, please, Lord, plunge me into your heavenly waters. Drown me in them; drown my passions, my pride, and all my vices and faults, that whatever in me comes from myself may die and the old creature be no more, and that there be nothing else in me than you.

—Venerable Francis Libermann (1802–1852)[8]

CHAPTER ONE

BURNING WITH ZEAL

Opening Prayer

O Mary, Star of Evangelization,
Intercede with your Son
to bring about in each of us
a renewed enthusiasm for our faith.
Inspire in us the courage and zeal to live the Gospel
and to bring Christ to everyone we meet.
Open our hearts to the gift of the Holy Spirit,
the agent of evangelization,
and enable us to transform the world
in the image of your Son.

O Mary, Star of Evangelization,
enlighten us with the radiance of your Son,
walk with us in faith,
strengthen us in hope,
and unite us in love
as we strive to become disciples in mission.

We ask this through your Son, Jesus Christ,
our Lord and Savior. Amen.

—"Mary, Star of Evangelization," Brother Claude Lane, OSB[9]

Opening Scripture

When [Jesus] came to Nazareth, where he had been brought up, he went to the synagogue on the sabbath day, as was his custom. He stood up to read, and the scroll of the prophet Isaiah was given to him. He unrolled the scroll and found the place where it was written:

"The Spirit of the Lord is upon me,
because he has anointed me
to bring good news to the poor.
He has sent me to proclaim release to the captives
and recovery of sight to the blind, to let
the oppressed go free,
to proclaim the year of the Lord's favor."

And he rolled up the scroll, gave it back to the attendant, and sat down. The eyes of all in the synagogue were fixed on him. Then he began to say to them, "Today this scripture has been fulfilled in your hearing." (Luke 4:16-21)

Mini-Witness: "I Can't Hear You!"

John encountered Jesus and the power of the Holy Spirit in a personal way during a college retreat. Intense joy prompted him to share his experience with his mom, dad, and siblings over and over again, until one day his exasperated mom said to him, "If you know Jesus so well, why don't you go talk to your cousin Jim? He's a drug addict. He lives in a filthy building downtown. And his mother is worried sick about him!" So off John went, a man with a mission and a thousand butterflies dancing in his stomach.

Jim stumbled to the door and greeted John with "What do you want?"

"I just want to talk. Can I come in?" John asked. As they settled into two decrepit chairs, John blurted out, "I came to tell you about how I met Jesus." Then he described his experience on the retreat weekend.

"I can't hear you," replied Jim.

"Maybe the drugs have caused hearing damage," John thought. So he spoke in a louder voice: "I came to tell you how I MET JESUS!"

"I can't hear you," repeated Jim.

"Boy, he is really in rough shape," John thought as he pulled his chair closer. Now he was just a few inches away from Jim.

But before he could speak again, Jim shouted in his face, "I can't hear you! I have hated you since we were kids! You always invited my older brothers to stay at your house, but you never once invited me." John stared at him and stammered, "Jim, I am so sorry for hurting you when we were children. Please forgive me."

"NO!" answered Jim, signaling that their conversation—and their relationship—was over.

Fifteen years later, on Christmas Day, Jim called to share the joy of his own conversion to Christ and his healing from addiction. Jim said, "You're the first person I wanted to tell, John, because it all started when you asked me to forgive you!"

Part One
God's Invitation to Have Zeal for the Gospel

The people who heard Jesus read in the synagogue were taken by surprise. What nerve he had, saying that the Scriptures had been fulfilled! His faith and zeal were apparent. His enthusiasm flowed from his earlier baptism in the River Jordan, the event that was the beginning of his public ministry. At his baptism, he was immersed in water and plunged into the depths of his Father's love for him. He experienced the power of the Holy Spirit flooding his soul and driving him outward to the whole world! Then the Holy Spirit sent him forth to share the Good News of God's love with everyone.

> Now when all the people were baptized, and when Jesus also had been baptized and was praying, the heaven was opened, and the Holy Spirit descended upon him in bodily form like a dove. And a voice came from heaven, "You are my Son, the Beloved; with you I am well pleased."(Luke 3:21-22)

Fortunately for each of us, the Good News did not stop with the earthly life and ministry of Jesus Christ. Joy at encountering God enkindles the gift of zeal over and over again. It is echoed in the lives of people like John and Jim and all those who overflow with joy from encountering the risen Christ. Now God wants to give you that same inner spiritual fire and a new boldness born of meeting Jesus and knowing the magnificent love of the Holy Spirit. It is not a feeling but a grace that will move you forward, bringing to fruition the seed of

God's love planted in the depths of your soul. Zeal for Jesus will empower you to share your faith with others. As the U.S. bishops wrote in a 1992 document entitled *Go and Make Disciples: A National Plan and Strategy for Catholic Evangelization in the United States,*

> Jesus Christ sends that same Spirit upon everyone who is baptized in his name. For we have all gone down into the water of Christ and have all been anointed to bring Good News and to be true disciples. We have all received his Spirit. This is not a Spirit of timidity or fear, but a bold Spirit of life, truth, joy, and grace.[10]

Jesus not only models zeal; he also promises this same gift to you so that you can "go therefore and make disciples of all nations" (Matthew 28:19). Just as he promised a new Pentecost to the apostles (see Acts 1), he promises you a new outpouring of his Holy Spirit, who is the source of zeal, compassion, and all the charisms that you need to evangelize. Like the disciples and apostles in the early Church, God will grant you as many "Pentecosts," or outpourings of the Spirit, as you need in order to share the Good News about Jesus with others in your daily life.

Popes and Bishops with Zeal for the Gospel

Pope Paul VI, in the landmark 1975 apostolic exhortation called *Evangelii Nuntiandi* (On Evangelization in the Modern World), encouraged us to have zeal for the gospel and to surrender to the whole process of sharing our faith with others. He encouraged us as individuals and as parishes to consciously choose evangelization: "Evangelizing is in fact the grace and vocation proper to the Church, her deepest identity. She exists in order to evangelize."[11]

Pope St. John Paul II was so filled with zeal for bringing Jesus to others that he embarked on 104 trips abroad, logging a total of 725,000 miles. He challenged us to undertake a "new evangelization," a proclamation of the gospel that is "new in its ardor, methods and expression."[12] And he made this appeal to the whole Church:

> The moment has come to commit all of the Church's energies to a new evangelization and to the mission ad gentes ["to the nations"]. No believer in Christ, no institution of the Church can avoid this supreme duty: to proclaim Christ to all peoples.[13] (Emphasis ours)

In 2010, Pope Benedict XVI echoed this invitation by announcing the creation of the Pontifical Council for Promoting the New Evangelization, tasked principally with "promoting a renewed evangelization in the countries where the first proclamation of faith has already resounded . . . but which are living through a progressive secularization of society and a kind of 'eclipse of the sense of God.'"[14] He also held a worldwide Synod of Bishops in 2012 on the New Evangelization.

Finally, Pope Francis, addressing the huge crowd in St. Peter's Square on the eve of Pentecost 2013, said,

> Jesus is the most important thing. I would like to take the opportunity now to make a small, but fraternal, reproach among

ourselves, all right? All of you in the square shouted out, "Francis, Francis, Pope Francis" . . . But, where was Jesus? I want to hear you shout out, "Jesus, Jesus is Lord, and he is in our midst." From now on, no more "Francis," only "Jesus."[15]

The U.S. Conference of Catholic Bishops has also called us to a new zeal for Jesus and for evangelizing, not only in the 1992 document *Go and Make Disciples,* but also in a 2012 document called *Disciples Called to Witness: The New Evangelization.* The bishops offer us a practical definition of evangelization:

> Evangelizing means bringing the Good News of Jesus into every human situation and seeking to convert individuals and society by the divine power of the Gospel itself. At its essence are the proclamation of salvation in Jesus Christ and the response of a person in faith, which are both works of the Spirit of God. (*Go and Make Disciples*, 10)

Both documents also offer suggestions and insights for cooperating with the Holy Spirit that can help stir up the fires of faith and help all of us surrender to the Holy Spirit as the primary evangelizer.

Zeal in Everyday Life

But how can all of us, everyday people who have no special training, become zealous evangelists? Harvey was a proud Italian-American from a non-practicing Catholic family. He worked ninety hours a week in the carpet business. He and his wife had an eleven-year-old son, a beautiful new home, and a garage full of late-model cars. But even with all these things, he still wasn't happy. A friend at work noticed his sadness and invited him to join our weekly Bible study at St. Joachim parish. Within two weeks of joining us, his mother died, his wife asked for a divorce, and his son was killed in a car accident. His personal suffering was so overwhelming that we referred him to Catholic Charities to get counseling and encouraged him to continue sharing with us in our Bible study group as well.

Over the next six months, Harvey went through a deep conversion to Jesus Christ and began to know the power of the Holy Spirit. He returned to the Church and the sacraments. His family and friends were stunned by his peace and inner transformation. During the following two years, he reached out to and brought thirty members of his family back to the Catholic Church.

Harvey's particular witness reminds us that zealous faith does not come easily. As St. Rose of Lima (1586–1617) once said, "Let them know that the gifts of grace increase as the struggles increase. . . . This is the only true stairway to paradise, and without the cross they can find no road to climb to heaven."[16]

Spiritual Workout for Growth in Zeal: Conversion and Commitment to Christ[17]

For a variety of reasons, we Catholics often find it difficult to share our faith. One reason may be that we are out of touch with our own moments of conversion to Jesus Christ. This exercise is meant to help you reflect on your faith and consider moments when you became conscious of God's personal love for you. Becoming more aware of such moments in your life will help you avoid "spiritual amnesia" and will give you something to share with others.

Take a personal conversion inventory. In silence recall the events, circumstances, people, and experiences that led you to give your life to Jesus Christ. How were you evangelized? How were you brought into a relationship with Jesus Christ? Check all the statements below that apply to you.

I became aware of conversion and commitment to Jesus Christ:

- As a child (0–12 years).
- As a teenager (13–19 years).
- As a young adult (20–35 years).
- As a middle-aged adult (36–59 years).
- As a senior citizen (60+ years).
- It was a long, continual process over many years.
- It happened when I participated in a spiritual renewal experience (e.g., Marriage Encounter, Cursillo, Life in the Spirit Seminar, etc.).

- I gave my life to Christ at a large evangelistic rally/crusade/healing service.
- A friend/relative brought me closer to Jesus.
- I was reading Scripture or a spiritual book and decided to give myself to the Lord.
- A stranger introduced me to Christ as my Lord and Savior.
- I was watching television, a movie, or a video online.
- It was an instant conversion, like being struck by a bolt of lightning.
- I can't really say that I've been evangelized or converted to Jesus Christ. What must I do for this to take place in my life?

Use these questions to explore your initial response to Part One. Your reflections can be shared with a friend or in a small group setting.

1. What is your understanding of conversion? How important is it for you and for the Church?

2. Which one of the above instances is most meaningful for you right now? Why?

3. How would you describe your most meaningful experience of conversion to a friend? How would you share what happened with a young person? How would these descriptions be the same? How would they differ?

Part Two
Gifted with Missionary Zeal

Jesus tells us, "As the Father has sent me, so I send you" (John 20:21). Through Baptism, Confirmation, and the Eucharist (the sacraments of initiation), we are gifted with the Holy Spirit and sent to continue Jesus' evangelizing mission. We are invited to bring the Good News of Jesus into our families, living situations, neighborhoods, communities, parishes, and workplaces. But how can we be filled with zeal if we know only part of the Good News? How can we share our faith if we have gradually "downsized" who Jesus is? How can we go forward with enthusiasm and zeal if we have never heard or lived the whole message of his coming? The answer is simple: we can't!

"The Gospel can only be transmitted on the basis of 'being' with Jesus and living with Jesus the experience of the Father, in the Spirit; and, in a corresponding way, of 'feeling' compelled to proclaim and share what is lived as a good and something positive and beautiful," according to the *Lineamenta,* the working document prepared in advance of the 2012 Synod of Bishops on the New Evangelization.[18] And so we ask for the gift of zeal as we pray and before we care, share our faith, or dare to invite others.

Awareness of the Gospel Message

The word "gospel" literally means "good news" and revolves around who Jesus Christ is and what he has done for us. In Scripture, it means sharing, retelling, and witnessing to the "message of all messages" or "the greatest story ever told." In the New Testament, the Greek word for "gospel" is *kerygma*. It means "the preaching or proclamation of the events of salvation in Jesus." The second shorthand version of the Good News is in Philippians 2:11, which reads, "Jesus Christ is Lord." Still another important version is contained in our baptismal vows, which we renew every year at Easter. And finally, both the Apostle's Creed and the Nicene Creed are more expanded gospel summaries.

One way to make the Good News, in its entirety, your own is to use the acronym "GOSPEL." This memory device describes the Good News of new life and salvation given to us by God the Father through Jesus Christ his Son and lived out by the power of the Holy Spirit, who is at work in each of us and in the life of the Church. All of these declarations are meant to be re-lived again and again in the life of the disciple.

G is for *God* the Creator, who loves us unconditionally and wants our happiness (see 1 John 4:7-8).

O is for *ourselves,* children of God who have sinned (see Genesis 1:26-27).

S is for our *Savior,* Jesus Christ, sent to redeem us (see 1 John 4:9-12 and John 3:16-17).

P is for *Pentecost* and the *promise* of power from the Holy Spirit, who helps us turn from sin and selfishness to believe in Christ and to share our faith with others (see Acts 1:8 and Luke 24:49).

E is for *everyday entry* into new life, the decision to make Jesus the center of our personal and communal lives (see Acts 2:37-41 and Colossians 3:1-4).

L is for the *local* body of Christ (see Acts 2:37-47 and Ephesians 3:21) and for *liturgy* (the public worship of the Church), through which we grow in Jesus. This includes prayer, study, the sacraments, community, service, and evangelization.

You may find it helpful to memorize these six points so that you can stay focused on the gospel. You might also use these points to assess your own encounters with God and note which point might be the focus of a particular faith event in your life. For example, John's college struggle with depression might be focused on "S"—God sends a *Savior*. Therese might share her story about an all-night prayer experience as "P"—*Pentecost* of the Holy Spirit. (For an example of sharing a relevant part of the gospel message according to the needs of your listener, see "The Christ Story in China" in the New Evangelization Workouts section.)

Here is the way St. Benedict Joseph Labre (1748–1783) summarized the gospel:

Jesus Christ, King of Glory, came in peace. God was made man. The Word was made flesh. Christ was born of the Virgin Mary. Christ walked in peace through the midst of them. Christ was crucified. Christ died. Christ was buried. Christ rose again. Christ ascended into heaven. Christ conquers. Christ reigns. Christ commands. May Christ defend us from all evil. Jesus is with us.[19]

Trust in God's Presence in Others

We are made to be evangelized and to evangelize others. The *Catechism of the Catholic Church* opens with this statement:

God, infinitely perfect and blessed in himself, in a plan of sheer goodness freely created man to make him share in his own blessed life. For this reason, at every time and in every place, God draws close to man. He calls man to seek him, to know him, to love him with all his strength. He calls together all men, scattered and divided by sin, into the unity of his family, the Church. (1)

In other words, we are created with a God-sized hole in our hearts or, rather, a Trinity-sized hole. Jesus was sent by God the Father to fill that hole. This is the conviction that makes zeal possible. When you share your faith, you are not offering something that is foreign or irrelevant. Through you, God is offering what is most needed in the deepest part of another person's soul. Evangelizing is actually a part of God's plan to reveal love with a capital "L." It is a privilege and a gift. It is a way of offering the gospel with skin on it. God doesn't need us to do this but grants us the privilege of connecting others to Jesus, who is already wooing them to intimacy. As the *Lineamenta* for the Synod of Bishops on the New Evangelization emphasized, "The goal of the transmission of the faith is the realization of a personal encounter with Jesus Christ, in the Spirit, thereby leading to an experiencing of his Father and our Father" (11).

Look to the Saints as Zealous Evangelizers

When you lack zeal, look to the saints, especially the great missionary saints. Search for primary sources like letters and quotes by the saints themselves. For example, recall St. Peter's discouragement while fishing. Jesus responded,

"Put out into the deep water and let down your nets for a catch."
Simon answered, "Master, we have worked all night long but have
caught nothing. Yet if you say so, I will let down the nets." When
they had done this, they caught so many fish that their nets were
beginning to break. (Luke 5:4-6)

Then Jesus invited Peter to become a fisher of men (Luke 5:10).

Therese grew up in a faith-filled Catholic family. When she
was a toddler, she was healed of a clubbed foot during a visit
to the Shrine of St. Frances Xavier Cabrini in New York City.
When she was twelve, her grandmother gave her a brief biog-
raphy of St. Frances, which inspired her to serve Jesus. Later
still, as an adult, she continued to study and meditate on the
life of St. Frances Cabrini, especially by reading her travel diary,
which Frances wrote as she was bringing the gospel to at least
eight different countries.

Choose Missionary Discipleship

The gift of zeal is just one of many different gifts and charisms
given when you surrender more completely to the Holy Spirit and
ask to become a missionary disciple. The challenge is to acknowledge the Holy Spirit as a Person who loves you and who wants to
be your teacher, since the Spirit is the principal agent of evangelization. Ask to be filled and empowered for Christ's mission. Give
God permission to endow you with all the spiritual gifts you need
to reach out to others with the Good News. Each of us must, as
John Paul II urged, "allow ourselves to be filled with the ardor of
the apostolic preaching which followed Pentecost. We must revive

in ourselves the burning conviction of Paul, who cried out: 'Woe to me if I do not preach the Gospel!' (1 Corinthians 9:16)."[20]

Jesus Christ was sent into the world by God the Father in the power of the Holy Spirit. John's Gospel recounts that Jesus "became flesh and dwelt among us" (John 1:14, RSV), meaning that he "pitched his tent" among us. He came as *the* Missionary (Latin for "one who is sent"). He leapt across time, space, languages, age groups, and cultures to reveal God's unconditional love for us. His mission gave birth to the Church. And so we as his disciples are also sent, with no less of a calling than that of a foreign missionary who leaves his country and family for the sake of the gospel. And even though you might only leave your front door, when you step out of that door, you are sent out in the name of the Father and of the Son and of the Holy Spirit. That is why the last thing we hear at a Sunday liturgy is to "go and announce the Gospel of the Lord."

Spiritual Workout for Moving Forward: Obstacles to Sharing Faith with Others[21]

Many Catholics have a deep faith in Jesus Christ and the Church, yet they do not try to share their faith with others or get involved with parish or diocesan evangelization efforts. They may struggle with both spoken and unspoken obstacles.

What obstacles prevent Catholics in your family, neighborhood, community, parish, or diocese from sharing their faith with others? Rate the intensity of the obstacles below that you encounter in yourself and others. Circle a number under each obstacle on a scale of 0 (not an obstacle to evangelizing) to 5 (major obstacle to evangelizing). If you are using this exercise in a group setting, consider offering it to several people and sharing your findings (with confidentiality) at a later meeting.

- Belief that one's religion is a private matter.

    0   1   2   3   4   5

- Fallout from the sex-abuse scandals, including the loss of credibility of some Church authorities.

    0   1   2   3   4   5

- Inadequate knowledge of Catholic beliefs.

    0   1   2   3   4   5

- Uncertainty about how to share faith stories or the Good News of Jesus Christ.

    0   1   2   3   4   5

- Fear of rejection by peers if one tries to share one's faith with others.

  0   1   2   3   4   5

- Past experiences of confrontational evangelism or proselytizing with Christians or those from other religions, such as Jehovah's Witnesses or Mormons. (See the glossary on page 179.)

  0   1   2   3   4   5

- American value of pluralism: "Live and let live." "All religions are equal."

  0   1   2   3   4   5

- Pain from discrimination that Catholic parents or grandparents endured in this country.

  0   1   2   3   4   5

- Belief that one's good actions (attending Mass, kindness, etc.) are all that is needed to evangelize others.

  0   1   2   3   4   5

- Apparent failures at trying to share the Catholic faith with someone in the past.

  0   1   2   3   4   5

- Lack of a vibrant local Catholic parish where a newly evangelized person might go.

  0   1   2   3   4   5

- Belief that evangelization is too hard and takes too much work.

  0   1   2   3   4   5

- Belief that one's parish already is evangelizing others about Jesus Christ and the Church.

  0   1   2   3   4   5

- Another specific obstacle to evangelizing or sharing faith is
  _____.

0	1	2	3	4	5

Use these questions to explore your initial response to Part Two. Your reflections may be shared with a friend or in a small group setting.

1. What are your top three obstacles to evangelizing? If you are reading the survey as an individual, consider offering it to a friend or two. Then ask, "What seem to be the top three obstacles for all who took the survey?"

2. What obstacles are foreign to you (and to the people you surveyed)?

3. What obstacle seems most difficult to overcome? Why? What concrete step might you take to help yourself and others overcome one of these obstacles to evangelizing?

Closing Prayer

We suggest that you begin each day with this prayer for Christian renewal as a way of asking Jesus Christ for a deeper life in the Holy Spirit. If you do not feel as though you have a relationship with the Holy Spirit, use the fifty-day booklet of meditations called *A Prayer Journal for Baptism in the Spirit*, which includes this prayer:

> Jesus, I know now that I am Yours and You are mine forever.
> Thank you for sending Your Spirit to me
> That I might have the power to live this new life with You.
> Stir up Your Spirit in me. Release Your Spirit in me.
> Baptize me with the fullness of Your Spirit
> That I may experience Your presence and power in my life,
> That I may find new meaning in Your Scriptures,
> That I may find new meaning in the sacraments,
> That I may find delight and comfort in prayer,
> That I may be able to love as You love and forgive as
>   You forgive,
> That I may discover and use the gifts You give me
>   for the life of the Church,
> That I may experience the peace and the joy that
>   You have promised us.
> Fill me with Your Spirit, Jesus. I wish to receive all
>   that You have to give me.
> Amen.[22]

CHAPTER TWO

PRAYING: THE SPIRITUALITY

OF SHARING FAITH

Opening Prayer

O my God, Trinity whom I adore; help me to forget myself entirely that I may be established in You as still and as peaceful as if my soul were already in eternity. May nothing trouble my peace or make me leave You. . . . Give peace to my soul; make it Your heaven, Your beloved dwelling and Your resting place. May I never leave you, . . . my faith wholly vigilant, wholly adoring, and wholly surrendered to Your creative action.

O my beloved Christ, crucified by love, I wish to be a bride for Your heart; I wish to cover You with glory; I wish to love You . . . even unto death! But I feel my weakness, and I ask You to "clothe me with yourself" . . . to substitute Yourself for me that my life may be but a radiance of Your Life. Come . . . as Restorer, as Savior.

—"Prayer to the Trinity," Blessed Elizabeth of the Trinity (1880–1906)

Opening Scripture

"Do not let your hearts be troubled. Believe in God, believe also in me. In my Father's house there are many dwelling places. If it were not so, would I have told you that I go to prepare a place for you? And if I go and prepare a place for you, I will come again and will take you to myself, so that where I am, there you may be also. . . . I am the way, and the truth, and the life. No one comes to the Father except through me. If you know me, you will know my Father also." (John 14:1-3, 6-7)

Mini-Witness: Daddy's Not Here!

We pray for our children and grandchildren often, especially when it comes to their spiritual needs. When our oldest grandchild turned six, we prayed, "Jesus, please show yourself to her. Help Paige find her way to your altar." We prayed even though our request seemed to be impossible, since her parents weren't regular churchgoers at the time. But God listened.

During one of Therese's next visits, our daughter greeted her with a request. "Here's Paige's First Communion book. Can you do the first lesson with her, Mom?" So off went Therese with Paige and her two younger siblings trailing behind. The first lesson was about prayers like the Sign of the Cross and the Our Father. So Therese began demonstrating: "In the name of the Father . . . "

"Wait, Memere! Daddy's not here. Are we supposed to go get him?" interrupted Paige.

"No. We are talking to the Father of the whole world and all the people in it," Therese explained. She could see that this would take a while, especially when they got to the Holy Spirit. But her lesson was a small answer to our prayers. Later on, Therese also created a children's YouTube video called "How to Pray the Sign of the Cross," in case our grandchildren forgot this prayer.

Part One
God's Invitation to Pray

Prayer forges a link between our everyday life and God's presence in the same way that Paige was able to move from her experience of her daddy to God as our Father. It is also the first simple step to sharing our faith with others. Through prayer, God also opens the doors of heaven and ushers us into the Father's house, no matter what kind of fathering we may have experienced. But when you enter that door, do you forget yourself enough to pray for the people in your daily life? How do you pray for them? Do you present them to God as the subject of your complaints and worries, or do you work at cherishing them as sisters and brothers in Jesus? Do you pray that they come closer to God?

God's invitation to evangelize is first of all an invitation to pray. And more precisely, God invites you to move beyond your own needs in prayer. God invites you to give voice to the needs of others, especially their spiritual needs. Remember, our goal as believers is to lift one another up into the arms of Jesus, who is our final destiny and our greatest need. Our calling is to clothe ourselves with the heart and mind of Jesus as we are drawn up into the life of the Trinity, alongside those for whom we pray. This means bringing others to Jesus, person by person, day by day. It means grounding every personal relationship in Jesus, in the Father, and in the Spirit through prayer and then action.

We believe that God invites us to an even greater spiritual adventure, called evangelizing prayer, through which God converts us and changes our perceptions of the people around us. Evangelizing prayer allows Jesus to shape our hearts and grant us a greater sensitivity to the spiritual needs of others. Evangelizing prayer is the foundation for trusting in the Holy Spirit as the source of all holiness and transformation in ourselves and in others. Through this kind of prayer, we are made more effective signs of God's presence. And finally, the Spirit gives us greater zeal and hunger for God's intervention in our daily lives and in the lives of others.

Our long-term goal in evangelizing prayer is to become more teachable or docile to the Spirit in the context of the Church. Otherwise, our zeal and petitions will be unenlightened. Recall John's example of sharing his new life in Christ with his cousin. His sharing lacked the kind of sensitivity, repentance, and wisdom that are meant to be a part of sharing our faith with others.

Invitation to Conversion and "Amazing Grace"

Faithfulness in daily prayer keeps us on the road to lifelong, ongoing conversion. We move from being "lost" to being "found" by

Christ in a thousand different ways, from being "blind" to receiving new "sight" by the light of the Holy Spirit. As the U.S. bishops have pointed out in *Go and Make Disciples*, "This is crucial: we must be converted—and we must continue to be converted! We must let the Holy Spirit change our lives! We must respond to Jesus Christ" (14). This may happen in a day, a year, or a lifetime. Placing ourselves and others in the heart of God through prayer on a daily basis helps us to become established in God and makes us instruments of God's transforming love.

Some of us become instantaneously conscious of a dramatic call to turn from sin and follow Christ. Others become aware of God's promptings over a longer period of time, which may include more than a few detours. For those of us who pray daily, God's invitation to conversion is more recognizable and is often echoed by the challenging events of our lives. We recognize these events as part of God's invitation to a profound and radical transformation of mind and heart. We embrace God's direction for our lives through Jesus Christ.

Whether we take baby steps or giant leaps, movement toward deeper conversion to Christ will impart the gift of zeal for sharing Jesus and the gospel. So watch for God's constant invitations to conversion, and thank God for the small and large conversions that you see in yourself and others. Here are some transformations of the heart that you might recognize and rejoice over as you accept the Holy Spirit's invitation to move "from" old ways and "toward" new ways of seeing and living:

Kind of Conversion	From	Toward
Religious	Life as a series of problems and/or achievements.	Life as a mystery and gift, a journey with and toward God.
Awareness of God	Awareness of an impersonal force behind the universe.	Awareness of God and an invitation to a personal relationship.
Christian	[Partial] Knowledge *about* the historical Jesus and the commandments.	Encountering the Person of the risen Jesus as the center of our lives.
Ecclesial (Toward the Church)	Church as *they* and as institution and/or buildings.	Church as *we and Jesus* and as our spiritual home.
Emotional	Unruly feelings, self-centered and self-absorbed.	Unconditional self-surrender to God and to loving others.
Intellectual	Knowledge as a body of facts about the world, people, or God.	Knowledge as wisdom enabling us to think with Christ and the Church.

Here is an example of a conversion moment in Therese's life. Once, when John needed a new job, it became evident that he would have to widen his search beyond the state of Massachusetts. Therese was very upset at the prospect of leaving behind her family. She could not see beyond her feelings. So John challenged her to speak with God about how far she was willing to move. Therese took out a map of the United States and the struggle began. Finally, God gave her the gift of surrender. "Okay. I will go as far as the Mississippi, but no further." As it turned out, John's best job offer was at a parish on the shores of the St. Croix River in Wisconsin, which empties into the Mississippi just a few miles to the south. It was one of many emotional conversions in Therese's life.

Although praying for another person's conversion is part of evangelizing, it is important that we let go of our expectations and judgments about how and when that person's conversion might happen, as well as what kind of conversion is needed. This is something St. Monica (331–387) had to do hundreds of times while praying for her son, St. Augustine (354–430). For example, perhaps you experienced a moral conversion first, as a result of the promptings and prayers of a teacher, as John did in high school. Because of this experience, you might be tempted to think that everyone else should begin a relationship with God through a moral conversion. This is simply not true. So rejoice at what God has done in you first, and then let go and give God permission to transform others through any one of these kinds of conversion and in any order that pleases God. Remember, conversion is, by its very nature, a surprise that is given as a gift from the Holy Spirit.

Spiritual Workout for Growth in Prayer: Who is the Holy Spirit to YOU?

At Easter and Pentecost, we recommit ourselves to our baptismal vows, to ongoing conversion, and to the evangelizing mission of the Church: "Go therefore and make disciples . . . in the name of the Father and of the Son and of the Holy Spirit" (Matthew 28:19). But who is this Holy Spirit, who was so evident at Pentecost (Acts 2:1-12), especially in the astonishing conversion of the apostles and disciples? Who is this Holy Spirit that we invoke through the Sign of the Cross? Who is this giver of gifts, graces, and charisms in your everyday life?

Names or titles for the Holy Spirit in Scripture, Tradition, and Church teaching are listed below. Some can be used as prayers in and of themselves. Circle three to six titles that you find most meaningful.

Advocate * Comforter * Mighty Wind * Willing Spirit
* Water of Life * Gift of God * Healer * Breath of God
* The Presence * River of God * Consuming Fire * Soul
of the Church * Power of the Most High * Lord * Glory
of God * Breath of Heaven * Third Person of the Trinity *
Helper * Finger of God * Living Flame of Love * Cloud of
Unknowing * Counselor * Paraclete * Dove * Divine Seal
* Giver of Gifts * Spirit of Jesus * Holy Ghost * Anointing
Consoler * Light * Giver of Life * Spirit of Truth * Spirit of
Wisdom * Spirit of the Father * Sanctifier * Holy One *
Spirit of Understanding * Eternal Spirit * Kiss of God *

Oil of Gladness   *   Agent of Evangelization   *   Strength of God
  *   Voice of the Lord   *   Teacher

Imagine yourself at the first Pentecost, the birthday of the Church, when the Holy Spirit came down upon the praying disciples of Jesus and transformed them (see Acts 2). You might pray with hands outstretched, inviting the Spirit to fill you by using the words below from another part of Blessed Elizabeth's "Prayer to the Trinity." Then call out to the Spirit by adding the titles you have chosen to pray. Use one or more of these titles in the blank spaces below.

"Through all nights, all voids, all helplessness, I want to gaze on You always and remain in Your great light. . . . O consuming Fire, Spirit of Love, come upon me."

"Come, _____, fill my heart. Come, _____ , fill my life. Come, _____, bless my family. Come, _____, transform me."

End by slowly praying the Sign of the Cross.

Use these questions to explore your initial response to Part One. Your reflections can be shared with a friend or in a small group setting.

1. What is it like for you to speak to the Holy Spirit? Which two or three titles inspire you or are most helpful to you? Why did you choose these? Which of these titles is the most foreign to the way you envision the Holy Spirit? Why? Think

of one or two people in your life. Which title of the Spirit seems to describe the way they respond to God's Spirit?

2. How does your understanding of a favorite name for the Holy Spirit move you forward in the evangelizing mission of the Church? What steps might you take to engage in more evangelizing prayer for others?

3. What part has the Holy Spirit played in your own ongoing conversion? What kinds of conversion have you experienced? What kind of conversion do you most need right now? When have you prayed for the conversion of others? What was that like? What evidence have you seen of the Spirit moving someone closer to God?

Part Two
Gifted to Pray for Others

The simplest way to enter into the gift of evangelizing prayer is to ask for the grace to see someone from God's point of view. Choose a particular person with an immediate need. Describe his or her situation to Jesus. Ask God for what might be needed: a new job, a successful surgery, the mending of broken family relationships. Then allow these needs, however complicated or serious, to be a doorway for even deeper prayer. Tell Jesus that you know he wants to help. Then search out and surrender deeper spiritual needs, in the same way that a physician would X-ray someone for a broken bone before stitching torn skin. (The chart on page 47 might help.) Finally, pray often, asking Jesus to meet this person's greatest need of all—an awareness of the Father's care, the redeeming love of Jesus, and the unquenchable passion of the Holy Spirit.

When we pray this way, we join ourselves to Jesus, who is the great High Priest before the throne of God (Hebrews 4:14-16). We also open ourselves up to the charisms and gifts that God wants to give us for the sake of that person. For example, when Therese's brother Robert was diagnosed with stage-four cancer, she began praying by offering up to Jesus all his medical treatments. She gave God her own fears too. Then she asked God to show her Robert's deeper needs. This was difficult, partly because Therese and her brother spoke to each other only a few times a year, at best. "What can I do, God?" she prayed. Then she sensed God saying, "Why don't you be his sister and call him!" So she committed herself to calling Robert every Sunday. God's compassion and healing touched them both over the three years between his diagnosis and the time of his death.

Visualize God's Presence

You can enter into evangelizing prayer by meditating with a photograph of a person or by closing your eyes and imagining Jesus approaching this loved one, co-worker, or neighbor. Notice the affection Jesus has for that person, and imagine them embracing. Describe the person's need, and then listen for what Jesus might say. Christ is truly present when we ask him to come. Pray in this way until you can thank Jesus for the small ways that he is already active in this person's life.

Another way to pray is to imagine this person inside a building, perhaps in his or her home. Then imagine Jesus knocking at the front door, a door without an outside knob. Is the door locked or jammed shut? Is it rusted? Is it too heavy? Will your loved one open the door? Then imagine that something remarkable happens. All of a sudden, the condition of the door doesn't matter. As you pray, the risen Jesus goes through the door and puts his arms around your loved one. And the strength of his love gives your loved one the inspiration to open the door to a new life of grace.

When our daughter Anne was a college student, her apartment caught on fire. The flames stopped just a few inches from the homemade quilt at the foot of her bed, so our prayers began with thanking God that she was out of the house at the time. Then we visualized Jesus at the foot of her bed as the fire raged. During a visit later in the week, we found out that the fire chief had stood in that same spot and remarked, "I don't understand why the whole room didn't go up in flames. It should have!" As the days went by, we prayed that she would be able to replace her belongings and feel safe again. We asked God to enfold her in a new blanket of his loving kindness.

Who Do We Pray for?

Scripture uses the Greek word *oikos*, meaning "household," to describe the people with whom we interact on a regular basis, such as family, friends, co-workers, and even significant strangers. These are the people we pray for first so that we can reach out to them and choose them as brothers and sisters. Jesus did this when he reached out to the Samaritan woman at the well (John 4:3-42) and when he prayed with Peter's mother-in-law upon entering Peter's house.

> Now Simon's mother-in-law was in bed with a fever, and they told [Jesus] about her at once. He came and took her by the hand and lifted her up. Then the fever left her, and she began to serve them. (Mark 1:30-31)

So look around your circle of friends, relatives, co-workers, and acquaintances for people who might need God's touch and God's word. Choose a few individuals to pray for on a regular basis, and pray for their spiritual needs as well. Therese keeps a photo of our children and grandchildren on her nightstand so that she can place each one in God's arms as she wakes up. John finds himself praying for the janitors in his building and the people he eats lunch with in the cafeteria.

As you pray for others, pay particular attention to those who are not churchgoers or who have broken or sporadic relationships with God. Ask God, "Who is ready to hear about Jesus?" Then watch for God's invitations to share your faith. It is not always the most obvious people who are ready for a spiritual change, but it is often the people who are experiencing major transitions that challenge their beliefs: the death of a loved one, a new job, divorce, marriage, a serious illness, a disaster, a move, or financial difficulties. These circumstances are sometimes called "divine appointments," times when God's love is present in a special way. Ask for God's guidance in recognizing and responding to these needs.

St. Joseph Moscati (1880–1927), the first modern doctor to be canonized, prayed for his patients at daily Mass. He also took the time to pray with many of his patients. He told young doctors, "Remember that you have to deal not only with the bodies but also with the moaning souls coming to you." Through his attention to body and soul, he brought many people back to God and the Church.[23]

How Do We Pray?

Ask God to show you his presence in someone's life. Perhaps, for example, Michelle is upset about an argument with her husband. So you might begin by thanking Jesus that a brewing problem in their relationship has finally come to light. You might continue by asking, "Show me what Michelle needs most to know that she is loved, Jesus." It might be someone to listen to her troubles or clarity about what her husband needs. Whatever God shows you becomes the next step for more focused prayer and guidance for sharing with Michelle, in whatever way that God wants.

John uses another strategy. He begins his daily prayer with this request: "Jesus, please send someone into my day with whom I can share your love and your word. Help me recognize the opportunities you give me." It is this prayerful sacrifice of readiness that is important and instrumental in helping others come closer to God, even if all we do is notice someone who needs prayer. Alice tried this strategy too. When she did, she was very surprised at the idea that God might be sending her an annoying woman, named Grace, who came up to her desk at work every day. First, she asked God to forgive her for being inattentive and judgmental with Grace. Then, she prayed for the strength to listen to Grace every day. Over time the two became friends, and together they invited two carloads of people from the office to a healing Mass in Alice's parish. "Annoying Grace" had become "Amazing Grace" through the intervention of the Holy Spirit.

Respond to God's Promptings

Our ability to respond to God's leadings in prayer hinges on our growing sensitivity to the Holy Spirit's promptings and on learning and discernment within the context of a community of committed disciples of Jesus. "Being a disciple is a challenge," the U.S. bishops write in *Disciples Called to Witness*. "Fortunately, one does not become a disciple of Christ on his or her own initiative. The work of the Holy Spirit within the Christian community forms the person as a disciple of Christ."[24]

Therese remembers an example of being sensitive to the Holy Spirit in prayer while she was driving to Massachusetts to visit her dad. Her plan was to visit her Aunt Rosemarie on her way home a few days later. Rosemarie was in a rehabilitation center, recovering from an accident in which she had been struck by a car. The facility would be a good halfway stop on Therese's trip back to Long Island. But God had a different idea.

As Therese was passing the facility on the drive up, she prayed for Aunt Rosemarie and suddenly experienced a sense of urgency. "Go now!" she sensed God saying. So she pulled off the highway and went back to the facility. There she found Rosemarie in a hospital bed with her hips in a circular metal brace and both legs in casts with pins. Just moments after they had exchanged greetings, the nurse announced that it was time for Rosemarie's physical therapy. Today she would try to walk for the first time since the accident.

So Therese grabbed her coat and got ready to say goodbye. "Please stay!" was her aunt's response. So off they went together, Rosemarie to be hoisted up between parallel bars and Therese to pray. The beads of sweat glistened on Rosemarie's face as she took one agonizing step toward Therese. What a privilege it was for Therese to be a sign of God's loving presence, and it would not have happened without God's promptings. So let us pray with Blessed Pauline von Mallinckrodt (1817–1881): "Lord, help me be a soul of prayer; help me that all my works swim in prayer."[25]

Spiritual Workout for Moving Forward: Letting God's Word Evangelize YOU

According to Pope Benedict XVI, rediscovery of the ancient practice of *lectio divina*, the prayerful meditation or "divine reading" of Scripture, is crucial to the evangelizing mission of the Church. He encourages us to read Scripture prayerfully so that we might hear God speak and experience the kind of intimate dialogue with God that will open our hearts: "One must never forget that the Word of God is a lamp for our steps and a light on our path."[26]

So how can you let God's word evangelize you as a part of your prayer time? And how can you develop a greater sensitivity to the promptings of the Holy Spirit? Below are five simple steps that will help you establish a prayerful dialogue with God and enable you to experience the "divine reading" of the Scriptures.

Turn to the opening Scripture for this chapter or another short passage. You can choose a passage on your own, one from the daily Mass that day, or one from the upcoming or previous Sunday Mass.

1. *Pause*
First, relax and let go of the concerns of the day. Slow breathing for a minute or two is helpful, as are stretching exercises or closing your eyes. Some people relax by listening to Christian music or reading prayerfully from a saint's life or a short meditation. Then gently focus your attention on the Lord Jesus by slowly praying a formal prayer such as a Hail Mary. Or you

can pray one of the titles of Jesus, such as "Savior," "Brother," "King," or "Healer."

2. *Pour Over*
Read the passage you have selected. Pour yourself into the word of God like water poured to overflowing into a vessel. Get a sense of the passage as a whole by reading a short commentary or footnotes from the passage itself. Then read it again. Let the water of God's word pour over you, cleansing you from within. Let the living words cling to you and penetrate your being. Slowly repeat a word, a phrase, or an image that strikes you as meaningful or that lifts you into Jesus' presence.

3. *Ponder*
Enter a striking phrase in a spiritual journal with the day's date and the Scripture citation (such as "Matthew 28:18-19"). Paraphrase the verse in your own words. What does Jesus want you to receive from this passage? Then write down three possible concrete responses you might make to this message (e.g., pray longer, help someone in need, forgive someone).

4. *Pray*
Talk to Jesus or write a short letter as a way of surrendering your feelings to Christ. This clears the way for receiving further insights about your life. Rest in the silence of God's presence for a few minutes. Listen for God's voice and wait for his inner touch, however light or tenuous. Thank Jesus for what he is doing within you, whether you can perceive the action of his Holy Spirit or not.

5. *Proclaim*

As you go through the day, periodically refocus on the word, phrase, or image from your prayer in order to reenter Christ's presence. Watch for a way to share what you have sensed with a spiritual friend, spiritual director, or small faith-sharing group. You might even share the gist of it with a co-worker or acquaintance (without necessarily using religious jargon).

Use these questions to explore your initial response to Part Two. Your reflections can be shared with a friend or in a small group setting.

1. Which of the five steps above for praying God's word (Pause, Pour Over, Ponder, Pray, or Proclaim) is easiest for you? Why? Which of the five steps above is most difficult for you? Why?

2. How might the "divine reading" of Scripture help you connect with Jesus in daily life? How is he evangelizing you right now? Who might you share your prayerful connection with (e.g., a spiritual friend, spiritual director, church community, or small faith-sharing group in your parish)?

3. How might this kind of scriptural prayer equip you to share your faith with others? What part does formal prayer, surrender prayer, reading Scripture, or seeking the Holy Spirit play as you ask for God's help on another's behalf?

Closing Prayer

O Eternal Word, Word of my God, I want to spend my life in listening to You, to become wholly teachable that I may learn all from You. Then, through all nights, all voids, all helplessness, I want to gaze on You always and remain in Your great light. . . . O consuming Fire, Spirit of Love, "come upon me," and create in my soul a kind of incarnation of the Word: that I may be another humanity . . . in which He can renew His whole mystery. (From "Prayer to the Trinity," Blessed Elizabeth of the Trinity)

Glory be to the Father, and to the Son, and to the Holy Spirit, as it was in the beginning, is now and ever shall be, world without end. Amen.

CHAPTER THREE

CARING WITH THE
COMPASSION OF JESUS

Opening Prayer

Dear Lord, . . .
Flood my soul with Your spirit and life.
Penetrate and possess my whole being so utterly
   that all my life may only be a radiance of Yours.
Shine through me, and be so in me that every soul
   I come in contact with may feel Your presence in my soul.
Let them look up and see no longer me, but only Jesus!
Stay with me, and then I shall begin to shine as You shine,
so to shine as to be a light to others.
The light, O Jesus, will be all from You;
none of it will be mine.
It will be You, shining on others through me.
Let me thus praise You in the way You love best,
by shining on those around me.

—Blessed John Henry Newman (1801–1890)

Opening Scripture

Beloved, let us love one another, because love is from God; everyone who loves is born of God and knows God. Whoever does not love does not know God, for God is love. God's love was revealed among us in this way: God sent his only Son into the world so that we might live through him. In this is love, not that we loved God but that he loved us and sent his Son to be the atoning sacrifice for our sins. Beloved, since God loved us so much, we also ought to love one another. No one has ever seen God; if we love one another, God lives in us, and his love is perfected in us. (1 John 4:7-12)

Mini-Witness: Without a Fatality

We were driving back home to New Jersey after my dad's funeral in Worcester, Massachusetts. Therese and our youngest daughter were taking a nap as we approached a narrow overpass near New Britain, Connecticut. Our car was in the right-hand lane when a large truck, filled with 64,000 pounds of rocks, came bearing down beside us and turned into our car. John saw the side mirror being sliced off by the bolts in the truck's front wheel. Pieces were flying everywhere, and there was nothing he could do. He just held the steering wheel steady until both he and the truck driver could pull off at a nearby exit.

The state trooper who came to our assistance walked up to our car and said, "God must really love you!" We were so rattled that his words only added to our shock. He continued, "In all my twenty years of police work, I have never seen a truck like this tangle with a small car without there being fatalities. You should have flipped over the bridge's railing and landed on the highway below." Slowly we recognized the truth behind his words, and after a short rest, we were able to drive home because of his spiritual encouragement.

Part One
God's Invitation to Care

The opening prayer by Blessed John Henry Newman describes love and caring as flowing from the light of God's presence within us. The opening Scripture passage is very similar, saying that love is born from first knowing God's love. But how many of us know how to tap into the vast reservoir of God's loving presence as we serve others? How many of us take the simple step of grounding our care in prayer? How many of us go beyond our inner resources in the name of a loving Father who will sustain those around us? How many of us allow Jesus, who is the Father's compassion made flesh, to love others through us? How many of us surrender to the Holy Spirit's promptings about how to serve others? The state trooper we met is an example of someone who saw what God had done to protect us and then reached out to us with that awareness. He went beyond his official duties and stepped into caring for us in the name of Jesus.

We believe that you can do the same because of your unique baptismal relationship with God, no matter what your occupation is or how complicated your relationships are. God can use you to care for others, and he will do it with his own love flowing through you. Dorothy Day reminds us of God's immense love that is available to us when she writes, "Lord, I believe, help Thou my unbelief. My faith may be the size of a mustard seed but even so, even aside from its potential, it brings with it a beginning of love, an inkling of love, so intense that human love with all its heights and depths pales in comparison."[27]

The Holy Compassion of Jesus

The invitation to act from the depths of God's holy compassion is at the heart of caring in the name of Jesus. God's love is meant to be the pulse of our caring. Jesus himself, as well as his disciples, shows us how in the Scriptures, and we can also learn from God's saints, who moved beyond simple concern to become effective and radiant instruments of God's love. But keep in mind that "holy compassion" is not primarily about what you give or do but who you are in Jesus. What makes your caring become holy compassion is an ongoing vital relationship with God at work in your heart and soul. Holiness acts like a beacon for those in need around you. And the Holy Spirit grants you the fruits of the Spirit and the grace you need to grow in imitating Jesus and the saints. St. Paul echoes this invitation to a holy love:

> Let the same mind be in you that was in Christ Jesus,
> who, though he was in the form of God,
>   did not regard equality with God
>   as something to be exploited,
> but emptied himself,

taking the form of a slave,
being born in human likeness.
And being found in human form,
he humbled himself and became obedient to
the point of death—
even death on a cross. (Philippians 2:5-8)

Consider the many instances when Jesus stopped what he was doing because the needs of another called forth his compassion: the widow of Nain, whose only son and means of support had died (Luke 7:11-17); the woman with a hemorrhage (Luke 8:43-48); and Nicodemus, who came to Jesus with doubts and questions (John 3:1-21). Think about St. Peter after Pentecost. When a beggar asked for money, Peter replied instead, "What I have I give you; in the name of Jesus Christ of Nazareth, stand up and walk" (Acts 3:6). Can we see people's needs—especially those of our family members, who need a special kind of caring—through the eyes of Jesus?

It is precisely in the arena of everyday service that we can apply the message of Jesus most directly. The U.S. bishops wrote the following in *Disciples Called to Witness* to describe this important challenge of sharing our faith through caring:

Throughout his public ministry, the Lord Jesus welcomed the stranger, healed the sick, offered forgiveness, and expressed his eagerness to give rest to the weary and burdened. How do we, today, follow the call and summons of Jesus to seek out the stranger, heal the sick, and welcome the weary? (Part I)

Caring as an Act of Gratitude

The opening Scripture passage reminds us that "since God loved us so much, we also ought to love one another" (1 John 4:11). This implies that caring comes from an appreciation for how much we are loved. St. Frances Cabrini (1850–1917) says it another way in her travel diary: "Let us warm our hearts with holy gratitude, which in turn will inebriate us little by little with divine love." This does not mean that you will always feel grateful enough to care for others. It does mean that caring flows best alongside the gift of humility. It means that a good beginning is a prayer like this one: "I know that all I have is a gift. I know that God has given me more than enough energy, time, resources, and inner strength to take care of my neighbor. I know that the fountain of God's holy compassion is endless, no matter the difficulty. Use me, God."

But gratitude to God should not stop with recognizing your own gifts. God invites you to enter into his endless mercy and gratitude for each person in your life, even when it takes a lot of prayer and imagination to do so. God's recognition of each person's goodness and his compassion towards each person's shortcomings are meant to become your strength and your points of reference for what to offer others. When this happens, your caring becomes a way of honoring God's presence in your neighbor. And that neighbor's needs will call forth your gifts.

Consider the grieving Jesus at the tomb of Lazarus (John 11:38-44). He had already surrendered his friend to the Father from a distance (11:4). So now his prayer begins with gratitude to his Father for hearing him (11:41). Then he addresses

Lazarus (11:43). And now his friend's death calls forth the gifts of Jesus. Through this healing, both Jesus and Lazarus experience the compassion of the Father, who has given them back to each other at a crucial time in the life of Jesus.

Your grateful care for others can take many forms, all the way from a simple smile, to acts of loving kindness for your family, to stocking a parish food pantry, to works of social justice, such as writing letters to Congress. The list of possibilities is endless, and so is the fountain of God's love that can be unleashed through holy and compassionate caring. All you need is a willingness to be moved by compassion and gratitude as you apply God's unconditional love for individuals, for families, for communities, and for the world around you. All you need is an awareness of how God might use your gifts to lavish his love on those around you.

Spiritual Workout for Growth in Caring: Evangelizing Styles[28]

As we enter into God's love for another person, the Holy Spirit energizes a whole array of personal and spiritual gifts so that we can respond to others in love. God also offers fruits of the Spirit and charisms that go beyond our natural talents. Here are some common evangelizing styles, or clusters of gifts, that we might experience as we surrender to God's particular compassion for others.

Some of the saints share a common style of caring, a cluster of gifts that they used with God's guidance. Reading their lives more closely might also reveal the struggles that go along with each evangelizing style or cluster of gifts. First, read the following list and check off one or two styles of caring that appeal to you. Second, read the list again, this time with an eye toward which style is closest to your own way of caring. And finally, put these styles in order, placing a "1" next to the one that best describes you and a "6" next to the one that is least like you.

____**Servant Style:** characterized by selflessness and small acts of concern. An example would be Blessed Teresa of Calcutta (1910–1997). Another would be St. Martin de Porres (1579–1639), who established the forerunners of free clinics and soup kitchens for the poor. And there is Jesus himself, who washed the disciples' feet (John 13:1-20).

____**Invitational Style:** characterized by hospitality, enjoyment in meeting new people, and the ability to gather people together. St. Bernard (1090–1153), for example, persuaded thirty-one friends and relatives to join him in monastic life. A biblical example would be the Samaritan woman at the well after her conversion (John 4:16-30).

____**Relational Style:** characterized by sensitivity, compassion, and friendly conversation. An example would be St. Francis of Assisi (1182–1226). Another would be St. Theresa Margaret (1747–1770), who cared for elderly Carmelite sisters with great affection.

____**Witness Style:** characterized by the ability to tell stories based on everyday experiences and the capacity to connect with others. St. Philip Neri (1515–1595) used stories, jokes, and even juggling to preach on the steps of the cathedral. Another would be Pope St. John Paul II (1920–2005), who could easily connect to youth and crowds in any language.

____**Intellectual Style:** characterized by an inquisitive mind, an analytical outlook, and the ability to discuss God. St. Ignatius of Loyola (1491–1556), the founder of the Jesuits, would be an example, as would Edith Stein (also known as St. Teresa Benedicta of the Cross, 1891–1942), the Jewish professor, convert, and writer. A biblical example would be St. Paul, especially as he spoke on the hill in Athens (Acts 17:22ff).

____**Challenging Style:** characterized by strong convictions and bold statements. St. Catherine of Siena (1347–1380) admonished popes. St. John Vianney (1786–1859) spent more than twelve hours a day as a confessor who could read souls. A biblical example would be Peter and his address on Pentecost (Acts 2:14ff).

Use these questions to explore your initial response to Part One. Your reflections can be shared with a friend or in a small group setting.

1. Which evangelizing style and saints do you admire most among those listed? Who is another favorite saint, and what gifts do you admire in that saint? What approach to others inspires you? What could you learn about sharing God's love from your choice?

2. Which evangelizing style is closest to your own approach to others? Which one seems to be least suitable in describing you? What do your choices say about your particular call to exercise holy compassion toward others?

3. What Scripture story about the compassion of Jesus most impresses you? What is your understanding of holy compassion? What kind of obstacles might keep you from this kind of love?

Part Two
Gifted with Caring Compassion

Caring is the most common step you can take in connecting others to Jesus. It encompasses being truly present to others, befriending those in need, encouraging one another, serving with a readiness to share, and performing the acts of mercy and justice that are the fabric of daily life. It is in the arena of everyday caring relationships that we are called to become the most transparent witnesses to the loving presence of God, both as individuals and as parishes.

Therese remembers reaching the checkout counter in an office supply store. A new clerk, named Alfred, made a mistake with a coupon and got flustered when she pointed out the problem. After a three-way exchange with the manager, Therese concluded her purchase with "Good-bye, Alfred." "How did you know my name?" he replied. "It's on your shirt. I noticed because I have a friend named Alfred who is a very kind person. And I am sure that you will live up to such a great name." Alfred smiled. A potential setback in his early employment had been averted by the grace of God and a small act of compassion.

There are also many people who need many acts of compassionate caring over an extended period of time. Gail was one such person. When she came to our parish, she needed a lot of prayer and counseling because she had suffered physical, emotional, and sexual abuse in her life. Then, just a few short years after joining our parish, her husband died. Four years later, Gail lost a teenage son in a drug-related murder. We thought she would suffer a terrible setback, but instead she felt so loved by the community that she went to the prison and forgave her son's killer. When we marveled at her strength, Gail shared one of her favorite Scripture passages with us:

> Blessed be the God and Father of our Lord Jesus Christ, the Father of mercies and the God of all consolation, who consoles us in all our affliction, so that we may be able to console those who are in any affliction with the consolation with which we ourselves are consoled by God. (2 Corinthians 1:3-4)

Witness of Life

In his 1975 apostolic exhortation *Evangelii Nuntiandi*, Pope Paul VI used the term "witness of life" to encompass all the big and little ways of acting and loving that make up our daily lives. He wrote, "Through this wordless witness these Christians stir up irresistible questions in the hearts of those who see how they live. . . . Such a witness is already a silent proclamation of the Good News and a very powerful and effective one. Here we have an initial act of evangelization" (21, 22).

The importance of sharing our faith through holy compassion is also emphasized in the *Catechism of the Catholic Church* (2447). And the Congregation for the Doctrine of the Faith has said, "Above all, the witness of holiness is necessary, if the light of truth is to reach all human beings. If the word is contradicted by behavior, its acceptance will be difficult" (*Doctrinal Note on Some Aspects of Evangelization*, 11).

One strategy for offering a more effective "witness of life" is to respond with simplicity to the people around us as we go about our day. John likes to call this "evangelizing as you go," instead of "going out to evangelize." For example, our newly divorced neighbor, Harriet, lives in a small two-room basement apartment with three narrow cellar windows. When she moved in, all she could see was a barren strip of dirt beside her driveway.

But Harriet loves the outdoors and the sunshine so much that she transformed that strip of dirt into a garden paradise. She spent hours removing weeds and lugging wheelbarrows full of good dirt. Then she carefully planted an array of beautiful flowers around a turquoise birdbath. Her final project was arranging a stone border around this exquisite paradise. It took her a while to find several medium-sized flat stones for a spiral that would end at the birdbath. The last stone was the hardest to find. Its absence began to remind her of the nagging loneliness that came with her divorce.

Around that same time, Therese was away at a wooded retreat center and thought of Harriet when she discovered a stone that was just the right size by a path through the trees. "Harriet, I found this for your garden while I was praying for you at a retreat house," she explained. Harriet was pleased and ceremoniously placed it beside the birdbath. A few weeks later, we overheard Harriet giving a tour of her tiny garden to a friend. She ended her tour with this: "And this is my holy rock. When I sit in my garden, I look at each flower, then at the birdbath, then at my holy rock, and I find myself praying."

Befriend Those in Need

Following Jesus implies an inescapable duty to make ourselves the neighbor of every individual and to take positive steps to help our neighbors, whether that neighbor is an elderly abandoned person, a foreign worker who suffers from unjust labor practices, a refugee on the other side of the world, or a family member who needs forgiveness. Following Jesus means asking the Father to help us lay aside the impersonal nature of our culture according to the leadings of the Holy Spirit. Following Jesus means asking the Holy Spirit to awaken us and to remind us of the words of Christ in everyday life: "Just as you did it to one of the least of these who are members of my family, you did it to me" (Matthew 25:40).

Perhaps there is no better recent example of befriending the poor than Blessed Teresa of Calcutta. Several writers refer to an episode between Blessed Teresa and a reporter who accompanied her as she walked the streets caring for the sick and dying. He followed her as she brought the dying to her clinic, where another sister or a volunteer would stay by their side. After several days of caring for people who had maggots in their sores, the reporter said to Blessed Teresa, "I wouldn't do that for a million dollars." She replied, "Neither would I!"

No matter what form caring in the name of Jesus may take in your life, God will use you in ways that flow from your personality, your gifts, and your evangelizing style. You will become a sign of God's abiding presence, friendship, and forgiveness, and your combination of faith and compassionate concern will become a powerful witness on many levels. You will become, as one author said, "one beggar showing another beggar where the bread is."[29] The key is to rely on God, not ourselves, as St. Margaret Mary Alacoque (1647–1690) wrote in this prayer:

O Heart of Love,
I put all my trust in you.
For I fear all things from my own weakness,
But I hope for all things from your goodness.[30]

Serve with a Readiness to Share

During Holy Week at St. Lawrence Church, Fr. Rich encouraged his parishioners to befriend their neighbors and to watch for opportunities to share their faith with them. One woman named Eileen took his exhortation literally and invited her next-door neighbor, Sylvia, to Easter Sunday dinner. Sylvia was thrilled to have a place to enjoy a nice meal on this important holiday. As they began to feel more comfortable with each other, Sylvia commented, "I notice that every Sunday morning you go out around nine. Where are you headed?" Eileen smiled as she shared that their destination was St. Lawrence Church. "Why do you go?" asked Sylvia. "Because it completes my week," replied Eileen. She couldn't wait to share what had happened with Fr. Rich.

Eileen's experience illustrates a very important point about the witness of life that has also been repeated in several Church documents, including Pope Paul VI's *Evangelii Nuntiandi*:

> Even the finest witness will prove ineffective in the long run if it is not explained, justified—what Peter called always having "your answer ready for people who ask you the reason for the hope that you all have" (1 Peter 3:15)—and made explicit by a clear and unequivocal proclamation of the Lord Jesus. (22)

We will say more about how to go beyond a silent witness in the next chapter, and we will also consider ways to move on after missing an opportunity to speak about Jesus. So don't worry. Even professional baseball players only succeed at bat about 33 percent of the time, but these stars are more than willing to swing their bats anyway. It's part of the game.

Acts of Mercy and Social Justice

Scripture reminds us that faith, acts of loving kindness, and acts that promote justice function best when they are exercised together. This is why God calls us "to do justice, and to love kindness, and to walk humbly with your God" (Micah 6:8). This means that efforts at sharing your faith through compassionate caring might also include working toward changes in society and institutions. Caring might include simple, prayer-filled, and holy ways of addressing poverty and suffering on every level, either directly or systemically.

Consider Rose Hawthorne, daughter of American novelist Nathanial Hawthorne and a widowed convert to Catholicism. She "moved into a tenement in the poorest area of New York City, and began nursing incurable cancer patients. . . . She took them into her home, changed their dressings, bathed them and fed them," according to one account of her life.

Given that she was dealing with an illness which was considered loathsome and communicable, like leprosy, hers was an act of immense charity and personal heroism. . . . Keeping her focus on God, . . . in one of her newspaper appeals for funds, Rose wrote:

"I wish to serve the cancerous poor because they are more avoided than any other class of sufferers; and I wish to go to them as a poor creature myself."

Rose Hawthorne, writes Sr. Diana Culbertson, OP, editor of *Rose Hawthorne Lathrop, Selected Writings,* "could look at the social evils of her day and see them not merely as deplorable but as a challenge. . . . She was far ahead of her time in her thinking on and commitment to social justice."[31]

Spiritual Workout for Moving Forward: Multiple Needs of Inactive Catholics

Now let's apply what we are learning about compassion to the people who are the focus of many New Evangelization efforts. As mentioned in the introduction, a study done by the Center for Applied Research in the Apostolate (CARA) in 2008 indicated that only 23 percent of Catholics in the United States are regulars at Sunday Mass. Additional studies about Catholic beliefs and practices have also been conducted over the past ten years that indicate that many Catholics have drifted away from the Church for one or more of the seventeen reasons listed here. An awareness of these reasons can help us realize that another person's needs often come in clusters.

What at first looks like a simple question of convincing someone to return to church becomes a question of being a "spiritual first responder," willing to care on many different levels. The needs may be social, emotional, physical, and spiritual at the same time, so it becomes very important to ask God what kind of caring is appropriate.

Step One: Place a circle next to the top three reasons why people in your parish seem to have become inactive.

Step Two: Put a check next to any of the issues below that you have struggled with in your own faith life, even though you have remained active.

Reasons for Becoming Inactive

___Does not experience God's presence in the Catholic community.

___Does not experience warm, personal, caring encounters with Catholics in a parish.

___Has difficulty bonding with people who do not appreciate their culture.

___Sees Catholicism as being complex and unrelated to their lives.

___Has a weak Catholic identity in the first place.

___Believes that the Catholic faith and creed seem unrelated to daily life.

___Views themself as "spiritual, but not religious." Turned off by organized religion.

___Sees self as being on a private quest for personal meaning.

___Experienced hurt from clergy or lay Catholics.

___Came into conflict with Church teachings.

___Was misled by people who attack the Church.

___Is in a marriage not recognized by the Church.

___Is married outside of the Catholic faith (other Christian group or world religion).

___Does not come due to chronic sickness or advanced age.

___Became busy and did not take the time to get involved.

___Relocated (college, job, home, etc.) and never reconnected with a Catholic parish.

___Is unaware of a nearby Catholic community.

___Other specific reason_____.

Use these questions to explore your initial response to Part Two. Your reflections can be shared with a friend or in a small group setting.

1. Share your responses to steps 1 and 2 above. What underlying needs might be a part of the reasons you have chosen? What has kept you living as an active Catholic or brought you back to being an active Catholic?

2. How might you respond with the compassion of Jesus to someone with one of these reasons for being inactive in his or her faith? How might your own gifts come into play as you express concern about any of their underlying needs?

3. Spend a few minutes praying for someone you know who has become inactive. Picture that person in a favorite place. Ask Jesus to enter the picture and help him or her take the next step to get closer to Jesus and the Church, even if you don't

know what that step might be. Finish by thanking God for this person.

Closing Prayer

Lord, make me an instrument of your peace.
Where there is hatred, let me sow love.
Where there is injury, pardon.
Where there is doubt, faith.
Where there is despair, hope.
Where there is darkness, light.
Where there is sadness, joy.

O Divine Master,
grant that I may not so much seek to be consoled, as to console;
to be understood, as to understand;
to be loved, as to love.
For it is in giving that we receive.
It is in pardoning that we are pardoned,
and it is in dying that we are born to eternal life.
Amen.

—Prayer of St. Francis

CHAPTER FOUR

SHARING FAITH IN CONVERSATIONS

Opening Prayer

Christ with me, Christ before me, Christ behind me,
Christ in me, Christ beneath me, Christ above me,
Christ on my right, Christ on my left,
Christ when I lie down, Christ when I sit down,
Christ in the heart of every man who thinks of me,
Christ in the mouth of every man who speaks of me,
Christ in the eye that sees me,
Christ in the ear that hears me.

I arise today
through a mighty strength, the invocation of the Trinity,
through belief in the Threeness,
through confession of the Oneness of the Creator of creation.

—St. Patrick's Breastplate

Opening Scripture

Now on that same day two of them were going to a village called
Emmaus, about seven miles from Jerusalem, and talking with
each other about all these things that had happened. While they

were talking and discussing, Jesus himself came near and went with them, but their eyes were kept from recognizing him. And he said to them, "What are you discussing with each other while you walk along?" (Luke 24:13-17)

Mini-Witness: Jesus in a Briefcase

Several years ago, John met an old friend at a high school reunion. After they had gotten caught up on all the day-to-day news, John wanted to share what, or rather who, had become the center of his life. He told Greg about his experiences with Jesus and gave him a small New Testament. Greg was not a churchgoer, but there was something he found reassuring about John's story.

Day after day and year after year, Greg carried the unopened book in his briefcase. He took it with him from place to place and even from country to country. Then one night about ten years later, Greg found himself in a hotel in Bangkok, mulling over serious personal difficulties. As he opened his briefcase to take out a snack, his eyes lingered on the New Testament. He took it out, opened it, and encountered God's living word. Each day he read a few more pages. Little by little, he sought out people with whom he could share about Jesus, until finally he returned to the parish he had left fifteen years earlier. The following Christmas he called John to share his story.

Part One
God's Invitation to Share Our Faith

God does not ask us to share our faith without also showing us how, when, and where. And God does not empower us to take this third simple step without giving us the companion gifts of discernment, self-surrender, and pastoral courage. This is especially true when it comes to faith-filled conversations. So let's look at the conversation between Jesus and his disciples on the road to Emmaus (Luke 24:13-35). In the beginning, Jesus did a lot of listening. He respected their experience of disbelief, and he was patient with their confusion and was willing to be invisible for a time. Now consider the conversation between John and Greg (which can also be called a witness). John did not pace the floor waiting for a call from Greg. He simply prayed for him from time to time.

When we read the New Testament, we realize that Jesus continually encountered dozens of people who weren't sure about his identity or about the Father's kingdom. And he engaged them with the Good News in many forms: stories, analogies, explanations, and healings. God's word is a living, spiritual reality that beckons rich and poor alike through the words of Jesus the Christ. So how can we do less than imitate the patient willingness of Jesus to speak? How can we do less than give the Father's message away, even if it remains dormant in a briefcase or in a companion's heart? How can we refuse to let the word of God take flesh in our hearts and on our lips, the same lips that we sign with the cross before we hear a Sunday Gospel?

Think about a time when a phrase from a Sunday hymn or from a Scripture reading lingered in your mind and brought great peace. These words that God whispered to you in prayer and in song are like a haunting refrain that you feel compelled to repeat. But quite often, these phrases are also prophetic words that have been underlined by the Holy Spirit. And furthermore, what if these words are not just for you? What if you are called to give voice to what Jesus tells you and what you see of God's presence by sharing your faith with others, just as Jesus did?

Such sharing happens naturally during a Bible study or faith-sharing session where stories and conversations about Christ are the norm. But are you willing to share these same stories of faith with friends, co-workers, and acquaintances in daily life? Do you realize that your faith in Jesus is portable and can be carried into everyday conversations according to the needs of those around you? Or do you save this kind of sharing for close spiritual friends who you know won't reject you? As God invites you to evangelize, you will find that small faith-sharing gatherings begin to function as practice sessions for sharing about Jesus in everyday life.

Jesus Listened with His Heart

Our friend Fr. Tony Krisak summarized a number of ways to imitate Jesus as we listen and speak with others, especially when we share about the important issues in their lives. So let's look to Jesus as a model of meaningful conversations as we consider Fr. Tony's suggestions:[32]

1. Jesus listened with his heart, and so can we. Imagine all that Jesus and Nicodemus must have said to each other before the challenging climax of their conversation in John 3:1-21.

2. Jesus spoke from his heart. He took the stance of a friend who refrained from judgment and listened to another's story. On the walk to Emmaus, for example,

   > [Jesus] said to them, "What are you discussing with each other while you walk along?" . . . Then one of them, whose name was Cleopas, answered him, "Are you the only stranger in Jerusalem who does not know the things that have taken place there in these days?" He asked them, "What things?" (Luke 24:17-19)

3. Jesus sought to make a connection with others. He did this by discussing the Scriptures with the disciples on the road to Emmaus. But he also attempted a connection with the rich young man (Matthew 19:16-22), with the thief on the cross beside him (Luke 23:32-43), and with the woman at the well (John 4:4-42).

4. Jesus focused on dialogue during person-to-person exchanges and kept debate for public conversations. One example is the man with a partial healing of his eyes (Mark 8:22-26). "Can you see anything?" Jesus asked (8:23). Then he continued his prayers without debating why the man was blind. Sharing our faith does not usually begin with an argument about religious practices or with an unsolicited explanation of doctrine.

Attention to Context

Matthew's Gospel, in particular, speaks about Jesus as the fulfillment of prophecies from the Old Testament. For example, in the genealogy of Jesus, the Evangelist refers back to Isaiah 7:14 when he writes, "Look, the virgin shall conceive and bear a son, and they shall name him Emmanuel, which means, 'God is with us'" (Matthew 1:23). What Jesus said and did was in the context of mankind's unfolding salvation history. And even though Jesus is the climax of this history, the story continues. Salvation history does not stop with Jesus, or even with the early history of the Church. Salvation history continues in our day and will go on past the time when we take our last breath—and we each have a unique part to play in it.

So how do I discern what part I am to play? How do I watch for and respect another person's spiritual journey as well as my own? How do I watch for ways our personal faith journeys might come together, even if it is for a brief moment? How do I surrender to the Holy Spirit's urgings and engage in faith-filled dialogue that allows both salvation histories to come forth? The place to begin is with asking yourself questions about your own spiritual journey. When did it begin? What are the high and low points in your story? Where is God in your life now? Your responses will give you new freedom and clarity. Remember, your story has the power to shed light on the Good News of Jesus Christ in a way that cannot be duplicated. So pray that your life story will be quickened by the Holy Spirit and that your words will act as a new Pentecost in the lives of those who are hungry for God's word.

Sharing faith stories with inactive Catholics, in particular, also begins with a respect for them as our sisters and brothers through Baptism. Each baptized person has Jesus as a companion, redeemer, healer, and Lord along his or her spiritual journey, whether or not this person has the religious language to describe that journey and whether or not Jesus seems to be invisible in their lives. You are called to listen for bits of another person's salvation history and to encourage its telling. God will help you be an attentive companion, like Jesus on the road to Emmaus. And like Jesus, you will see God touch hearts: "They said to each other, 'Were not our hearts burning within us while he was talking to us on the road, while he was opening the scriptures to us?'" (Luke 24:32).

We once took a very long cab ride across the city of Detroit to visit the shrine of Venerable Solanus Casey (1870–1957). When the driver asked us our destination, he told us that he once had a relic of Solanus. It had been a great consolation to him during many difficulties, but he had lost it one day when his wallet was stolen. When our visit ended, we requested the same driver, and during our return trip, we gave him a new relic. He was visibly touched by this kindness. Then his response was to share, on a deeper level, about his impending divorce. Near the end of the ride, we asked if we could pray with him and then joined him in an Our Father.

Spiritual Workout for Growth in Faith Sharing: Beyond a Wordless Witness

When our love and service to others is in tune with God's love, a new gift of intimacy is given, and new opportunities for sharing meaningful conversations arise. Our lives become an embodiment of the Good News. The witness of life is wedded to the witness of words.

Disciples of Jesus are called to share openly about the ways in which Scripture, prayer, and Catholic teaching connect with our life experiences—at home, in our neighborhood, in the workplace, and in church ministry settings. As Pope Paul VI wrote in *Evangelii Nuntiandi*, "The Good News proclaimed by the witness of life sooner or later has to be proclaimed by the word of life. There is no true evangelization if the name, the teaching, the life, the promises, the kingdom, and the mystery of Jesus of Nazareth, the Son of God are not proclaimed" (22).

Think about these common ways to share your faith with others. Think about how often you take the following opportunities to share faith. Place the appropriate letter next to each item: "N" for never; T" for two to six times a year; "M" for monthly; or "W" for weekly.

___ I meet with a spiritual director or advisor to talk about my relationship with Jesus Christ and how I might grow in the spiritual life.

___ I am part of a small group (three to eight participants) that meets regularly to share faith on a topic or question.

___ I participate in adult faith formation classes where we spend time sharing our faith in small groups.

___ I am in a regular faith-sharing relationship, in person or on the Internet, where we share our faith stories on a person-to-person basis.

___ I am part of a ministry or committee whose members share their faith stories as part of our regular meeting format.

___ I attend large meetings/events where I get the opportunity to share my faith stories.

___ I keep a notebook, journal, or blog in which I record my experiences with Jesus Christ and the Church in everyday life.

___ I teach classes where I get the opportunity to share ways that my faith connects with daily life.

___ I serve on a ministry or team from my parish/diocese that goes to homes, public places, or events looking for opportunities to share stories of faith with the people we meet.

___ I take advantage of everyday opportunities to pray with people who tell me about stresses, transitions, or needs that they are experiencing in their lives.

___ I share brief words of prayer with others through social media.

Use these questions to explore your initial response to Part One. Your reflections can be shared with a friend or in a small group setting.

1. What two or three faith-sharing practices do you engage in the most? Why? What two or three faith-sharing practices do you engage in the least? Why?

2. When and how have you recorded some of the ways that God has been present in your life so far? What are your plans for the faith stories you have written or recorded?

3. When someone shares a problem or asks for prayer, what is your usual response? How might you respond differently after reading this chapter? How might you show respect for ways that God has been with that person so far?

Part Two
Gifted by God to Share Faith

Some people agonize over questions such as these: Do I share my faith story with Joe? Do I talk to my son Ethan about going to Mass? Should I pray with Aunt Agnes, who has cancer? Will someone reject me if I speak about God?

When you find yourself asking such questions, here are a few suggestions. First of all, stop what you are doing for a moment and pray for this person. Remember, prayer is the first act of evangelization. Second, take a good look at your relationship with this person. Are you doing what you can to be an open and caring witness to Jesus?

Finally, consider some of the following options for a faith-filled conversation: asking questions about life, sharing statements of faith, telling faith stories, or praying with someone.

Pursuing Questions about Life

We have included an exercise in the New Evangelization Workouts section (see page 149) that describes several occasions when you might share your faith. They include times when a person is asking questions about the meaning of life or reminiscing about their childhood parish or their First Communion. Or perhaps they have just visited religious websites or watched Catholic events like a papal visit or election. These are just a few of the opportunities for bringing a conversation to a deeper level. This is not difficult to do. You might want to practice asking specific questions with a friend, such as "Would you like to say more about this?" or "What does this mean for you?" Then listen. You can also ask, "What do you make of all this?" or "What is your greatest need right now?" Or for someone who seems to know God, you can ask, "Where do you see God in this?" or "What do you expect of God right now?" A good question for someone who is complaining about God might be one of these: "And what do you think God's reply might be?" or "What has been your worship experience up to this point?"

Therese answered the door one day to find a young Jehovah's Witness named Brenda, who wanted to come in and talk.

And since Therese had been praying for an opportunity to witness, she said, "Sure, if you will answer one question for me after you share."

"Okay," was the answer. They got comfortable and Therese listened carefully. Then she asked her question: "Tell me, how did you decide to become a Jehovah's Witness?"

"Well, I guess it all started when I was about twelve. I used to be Catholic, until my grandmother died and the priest told my grandfather he couldn't go to Communion at her funeral. My whole family stopped going to church after that," explained Brenda.

In response to all the pain and the perceived offense behind her story (whether it was correct or not), Therese said, "I am so sorry." Then Brenda burst into tears.

Sharing Statements of Faith

The *Lineamenta*, prepared for the Synod on the New Evangelization, reminds us of this: "The Christian must never forego a sense of boldness in proclaiming the Gospel and seeking every positive way to provide avenues for dialogue, where people's deepest expectations and their thirst for God can be discussed" (5).

The simplest way to evangelize through words is to pepper our conversations with "spiritual one-liners," which consist of prayerful statements that can be taken from the creed, Scripture, the liturgy, and our own spiritual history. St. John the Baptist uses such a brief statement of faith in John 1:36 when he calls Jesus the "Lamb of God." Other examples of such prayers are "God loves you," "Peace be with you," "The Lord

·

is my shepherd," "Thanks be to God," "Lord, have mercy," "Glory to God," and "Alleluia!" If we first make these one-line prayers and declarations a part of our daily prayer, they will flow naturally into our conversations.

For example, you can say "God bless you!" instead of "Bless you" when someone sneezes. When we use these mini-sharings, we offer nuggets of religious language and imagery, which most unchurched and inactive people are lacking. We might also awaken spiritual curiosity in someone's heart. Using these one-liners might open the door to conversations about God. And finally, if a person were to read Scripture or visit a liturgy at a later date, these faith statements would be familiar connections to what is then happening.

Telling Faith Stories

Share a faith story from Scripture, from a saint's life, or from a time when you experienced God in a similar situation. But choose an episode that can be easily understood by the particular person. For example, "Your situation reminds me of the time that Peter wanted to walk on the water to get to Jesus." If you share an event from your own life, remember to share your experience of God, not your spiritual achievements. Better yet, share your failures in following Jesus and the ways in which God reached you at that time (when appropriate). And remember to avoid exaggeration or the use of religious jargon—words that only active Catholics would understand. If a faith story arouses a response, then you can continue the conversation together. If not, then simply foster more dialogue about that person's situation.

John was more than a little disoriented as he shuffled his notes on the podium. The extraordinary events of that past week still fluttered in his mind like a flock of excited chirping birds. Two days before, our son Stephen had been born. Because Therese's labor had been so short, an unfamiliar obstetrician had attended the birth. Now it was time to lay aside his excitement and teach a group of parents about prayer in the home. As John finished speaking, a gentleman stood up with a request: "Can you give us an example of prayer in everyday life?"

"Yes, I can," said John. Then he proceeded to share about praying with Therese in the delivery room when Stephen arrived. The more details John provided about the quick delivery at the hands of the doctor who happened to be on call, the more quizzical the man became. John finished by asking, "Does that answer your question?" "Why yes," Dr. Fitzgerald replied with a grin. "Now I know what you mean. I was there. I was the doctor!"

In this example, there was a clear indication that the time was ripe for sharing. But it is not usually that obvious. Sherry Weddell, director of the Catherine of Sienna Institute and author of *Forming Intentional Disciples,* offers some helpful guidelines for entering an open-ended dialogue about life's questions, or what she calls a "threshold conversation."[33] The most important guideline is to build a "bridge of trust" in the context of an ongoing relationship with the person you are evangelizing. Another is to trust God with the fruits of your conversation by giving someone a chance to think between one conversation and the next.

Therese had been calling her brother Robert every Sunday afternoon after he was diagnosed with cancer. The only difference on this particular Sunday was that it was Easter. So Therese described the Easter Vigil and the adventure of huddling together in the dark outside the church against a cold wind. One gust even caught a flame of the bonfire, threatening to lick Fr. Pat's sleeve as he lit the Easter candle. Then she described the procession behind the light of Christ and into the darkened church. After she finished sharing this highlight of her week, Robert responded, "They really do that at church? Gee, maybe I should come back!"

This conversation was one of only half a dozen over three years of weekly conversations that could be called sharing faith. But when Robert died a year later, it was one of Therese's greatest sources of consolation. Because of their exchange, Therese has hope that God has honored her brother's desire to come closer to the light of Christ.

Pray with Me, Please!

Pope St. John Paul II had a habit of praying aloud with a person, especially if he or she asked for prayer about a particular need. So did Venerable Solanus Casey, who was a porter in a monastery. Hundreds of people came to experience the grace of simple prayer with Fr. Solanus. This kind of faith sharing brings a person into God's infinite loving presence.

Here is one approach. First, ask the person's permission to pray together. Then, simply talk to God aloud: "Jesus, please come and help _____. I know you love her. We place her situation in your hands, and we will watch for your help." Be sure to leave a moment of silence. You can conclude with an expression of gratitude and confidence. "Thank you, God, for hearing us and for helping _____. We know your loving kindness is without end." Finally, ask the person what was happening as you prayed, and listen carefully to the answer. An alternative is to use a formal prayer like the Our Father. If a serious concern has been expressed, you might follow up with a phone call or text several days later.

Keep in mind that it is not the end of the world if someone refuses an invitation to pray. You can still bring the concern to God in prayer later on. When you do so, the Holy Spirit may invite you to change something in yourself or in the relationship that might be an obstacle to sharing faith through prayer. For example, God might prompt you to have a greater trust in Jesus or to let go of judgments about the person. If you pursue what needs changing by attending to your own conversion, you will become a more humble disciple and a more willing instrument of God's voice. Asking God to remove obstacles in us also helps us avoid the use of force or emotional manipulation.

Spiritual Workout for Moving Forward: Strengths and Weaknesses in Sharing Faith[34]

Ever find yourself sharing news about an important event in your life with several people? You think nothing of making lots of phone calls about a pregnancy, a new job, a decision to move, or an illness. Or you might post your news on Facebook, send a text, or even write a letter. You already know how to share big news. But if you listen to yourself tell and retell a story, you will discover that you have a certain style for sharing your news. The very unique skills you have are part of God's gifts to you as you share your faith.

Getting in touch with the kind of gifts you have for sharing with others is very important because God uses these same gifts as a foundation for sharing on a spiritual level. Then he anoints them with the gifts of his Holy Spirit to touch the hearts of others. Place the letter representing your **present** *skill or ability level in the space before each number below.*

A. No ability   B. Low ability   C. Moderate ability   D. High ability

___Ability to establish rapport, friendship, and a hospitable climate for sharing meaningful events and faith with others.

___Ability to identify someone's needs, problems, current spirituality, and level of conversion or faith development.

___Ability to present a silent witness to my faith through my lifestyle. In other words, I practice what I believe.

___Ability to verbalize what my faith in God means to me and how it has changed or affected my life.

___Ability to discuss the basic central truths of the gospel.

___Ability to invite another person into a deeper relationship with Jesus Christ.

___Ability to pray with a person who is seeking a new or deeper relationship with Jesus Christ.

___Ability to provide such a person with immediate follow-up (e.g., referral to a priest, counselor, social worker, or community agency, if needed).

___Ability to invite and include a person into my parish faith community (if he/she is not already a member).

___Ability to introduce him/her to an appropriate small support group (e.g., Bible study, prayer group, young adults, separated/divorced, etc., depending on his or her needs).

___Ability to peacefully and joyfully share my faith with others in the ways that I can and not in the ways that I can't, according to my present life and parish situation.

___Ability to teach or train other Catholics in all the above behaviors.

Use these questions to explore your initial response to Part Two. Your reflections can be shared with a friend or in a small group setting.

1. Who is someone you admire for his or her ability to share important faith stories? What qualities does this person embody from the above list? How has this person brought you closer to God?

2. Which two or three skills or abilities are your strongest ones? Why? Which two skills or abilities do you most need to grow stronger in? Why?

3. What is your experience of people asking you for prayer? If you were to pray with a person right when he or she asks, how would you do it? Consider practicing this kind of prayer with a friend or using the "Praying with Someone in Time of Need" exercise on page 157 in the Evangelization Workouts section.

4. By doing this exercise, I have realized that my own ability to share faith is _____.

Closing Prayer
For the New Evangelization

St. John Paul II, you called all Christians to the New Evangelization. Through your intercession, help us approach the New Evangelization with a sense of enthusiasm.

Pray that we embrace the sweet and comforting joy of evangelizing, even at times when proclamation might seem like a seed sown among tears. May it mean for us—as it did for the apostles, for the early Christians, for you, and for a multitude of splendid evangelizers all through the Church's history—an interior enthusiasm that nobody and nothing can quench.

And may the world of our time, which is searching, sometimes with anguish, sometimes with hope, be open to receive the Good News not from evangelizers who are dejected, discouraged, impatient or anxious, but from ministers of the Gospel who have first received the joy of Jesus Christ, whose lives glow with fervor, and who are willing to risk their lives so that the kingdom may be proclaimed and the Church established in the midst of the world. Amen.

St. John Paul II, pray for us.[35]

CHAPTER FIVE

DARING TO OFFER INVITATIONS

Opening Prayer

Let your voice sound within me, that I may understand what you want of me. . . .

Let your voice sound within me, and I shall go even to the farthest end of the earth, to do all that you ask, because the sound of your voice performs wonders.

In your name, Jesus, and enclosed within your Heart, I can do anything!

—St. Frances Cabrini[36]

Opening Scripture

The next day John [the Baptist] again was standing with two of his disciples, and as he watched Jesus walk by, he exclaimed, "Look, here is the Lamb of God!" The two disciples heard him say this, and they followed Jesus. When Jesus turned and saw them following, he said to them, "What are you looking for?" They said to him, "Rabbi, . . . where are you staying?" He said to them, "Come and see." . . . One of the two who heard John speak and followed him was Andrew, Simon Peter's brother. (John 1:35-40)

Mini-Witness: Lunch or Mass?

Therese's grandmother Jeannia needed assistance getting dressed, taking medicine, and using the bathroom. It was time for a nursing home. Unfortunately, she couldn't get into a Catholic nursing home where there was daily Mass.

At first she was disappointed, but as she settled in, Jeannia established a daily routine that revolved around a televised daily Mass and a Rosary at noontime. Over the years, she would invite anyone who missed going to Mass or needed consolation to join her. Her tiny room was always full. Then one day she told us, "Somebody threw a monkey wrench into our daily Mass!" Lunchtime had been rescheduled for noon. What would she do? And what about the other women who prayed with Jeannia in her room? That night they took a vote. Would it be lunch or Mass? It was unanimous—Mass was more important. It didn't take long for the staff to notice what had happed. In response, the head nurse ordered a special serving for the group in Jeannia's room at 12:30.

Part One
Recognizing God's Invitations to Me

We are humbled by the witnesses in these three opening pieces. We wonder who would have been concerned about the spiritual well-being of the women in Jeannia's nursing home if she had not been there. We are in awe of St. John the Baptist, who was willing to give away his disciples to his cousin, Jesus. And we can't even begin to count all the Italian immigrants in North and South America whose faith was enriched because of St. Frances Cabrini's willingness to follow Jesus to the ends of the earth. If you think back, you, too, can point to someone in your past who invited you, and even dared you, to believe in God and to belong to the Church. Who was this person? Was it a parent, a teacher, a grandparent, a spouse, or a friend? Was it difficult for this person to challenge you? What did it cost him or her? Have you thanked God for that person?

Ask yourself, "Where would I be if this person or persons had not offered me an invitation to believe?" Then move forward from an appreciation of the invitations you have received to an honest evaluation of the different kinds of invitations that you are willing to extend to others in return. You may be comfortable asking someone to a meal, a movie, a party, or on a shopping trip. But are you comfortable with inviting someone to Mass, a parish social event, or a parish volunteer opportunity? Why or why not?

When our youngest daughter began her studies in costume design, a friend gave us complimentary, standing-room-only tickets for the opera *The Magic Flute* at the Lincoln Center in Manhattan. Rose and Therese were so impressed with everything about the play and the costuming that they didn't even notice any discomfort from standing. Their gratitude went beyond words. And we were both inspired that someone was paying such close attention to our daughter's deepest desires. The experience prompted us to ask, "Do we pay attention to the spiritual desires of the people in our lives, especially the longings that can only be met by a faith community? Do we see liturgies and faith-sharing groups as magnificent gifts to be given away?"

The Challenge of Believing

Let's look at the basic invitation to faith. First, it's important for us to realize, as Fr. Tony Krisak has written, that in order to invite someone to faith, "we do not have to know everything about *what* we believe." However, "We do need to know *why* we believe or *why* we have faith. The 'why of faith' is much more easy to articulate than the 'what of faith,' as long as we give ourselves some time for reflection about why we have accepted the gift of faith."[37]

When we invite someone to experience faith, either as an individual or within a community setting, we also need to realize that faith is both a gift and a challenge. We are extending an opportunity to someone to say yes to the paradox of faith and doubt, yes to the cross of moving beyond self and into new life: "Yes, I trust what you are saying is true for you, and maybe later, it could be true for me as well." So even if you share with no strings attached, your words can still be very challenging.

Also, from that point onward, the offer of faith becomes a part of your relationship, like a spring that feeds into a lake. So it is important that you maintain the same good relationship you had before and rely on the grace of the Holy Spirit, who knows when to encourage and when to challenge the person you want to include in your faith community. The Holy Spirit also knows the length of time that someone needs to respond.

Finally, keep in mind that inviting others into a communal faith centered on Jesus is countercultural. You may be challenging others to move beyond what sociologist Grace Davies calls "belief without belonging." You may be nudging others to move past relativism (believing one religion is as good as another), spiritual individualism, or the false notion that sharing about God infringes on another's freedom. When you witness about your relationship with God, you are also inviting others to think about whether their personal "gods," such as money or prestige, are satisfying. Or you might be threatening the worship of self and the human body that fills gyms on a Sunday morning. Everyone (even you and I) is essentially like the rich young man who went away sad (Luke 18:23). There is a lot to let go of before a person can accept the richness of faith in the body of Christ and the peace that our Savior and brother, Jesus Christ, gives us when we gather together. So we rely on God to give this grace in his own good time.

Come and See

To offer evangelizing invitations effectively, your faith must be that of a missionary, a "holy madness" that inspires you to search out people, knowing that God wants to connect them with Jesus and the Church in some significant way (see Acts 4:29-31). Sharing your faith also means searching out those who are spiritually imprisoned and knocking at their inner doors with the invitation to come and see what God is doing among you. Sharing your faith means incorporating others into welcoming faith communities where the door is always left ajar for the stranger. And finally, your personal faith must draw strength from the Christian community, so that when you offer invitations, it is simply a question of inviting someone to join us on our journey.

For example, John's out-of-state cousin, Helene, phoned us out of the blue to say that she and her husband wanted to come for a visit the last weekend in the month. Unfortunately, we were scheduled to help out at a healing Mass that same weekend. Rather than viewing her request as an interruption, we trusted that in this case, Jesus was inviting Helene to the healing Mass with us. She accompanied us, and during the Mass, someone shared an insight with the whole assembly about a person who would be healed of a broken relationship with her daughter. "That's me!" Helene thought, even though she intended to seek prayer about her marriage. In the weeks that followed, she was reconciled with two daughters and then had the courage to deal with her difficult marriage.

Spiritual Workout for Growth in Inviting: Whom Can We Bring to Jesus?

Some of the most exciting New Testament stories about bringing others to Jesus involve what has been called "*oikos* evangelization." (The Greek word *oikos* means "household" or "extended family.") Many people heard the good news of Jesus Christ and then shared it with the people with whom they lived, worked, and worshipped.

Today we also function as a part of a primary web or network of relationships—an *oikos,* a community of people who share common locations, vocations, interests, social media, or kinship. We relate to others from within our households, workplaces, neighborhoods, communities, and social circles. One exciting development is that our *oikos* may also include online networks that reach across time zones and cover the globe.

The key to *oikos* evangelization is becoming more aware of the people around us and what Jesus is already doing in them through the loving presence of the Holy Spirit. This awareness equips us to evangelize as we go through everyday life!

For most of us, there are twenty to fifty individuals who compose our web of day-to-day relationships. They are in our family, at work, in our neighborhoods, and online. Some we communicate with daily. Others we come into contact with once a week or once a month. Create a list of three to six people in the following categories. To protect confidentiality, use first names only.

1. Family members with whom you have regular contact.

2. Co-workers that you interact with on a daily, weekly, or monthly basis.

3. Neighbors with whom you have regular contact.

4. Those with whom you share a common interest (friends, leisure activites, schools, organizations, clubs, or social networks like Facebook).

Use these questions to explore your initial response to Part One. Your reflections can be shared with a friend or in a small group setting.

1. Choose the first names (or give fictional names to maintain confidentiality if you are in a small group setting) of two people from your list who are going through times of need, stress, or transition. Note the reason why you chose each one. How open might they be to a conversation about God or an invitation to an event at your church?

2. What is your past experience of inviting people to a religious event? What are your wildest dreams about who would come and what would happen? What would it be like for you if everyone you invited to attend such a celebration replied with a "Yes"?

3. Spend some time praying in silence for each of the people above. Give the Holy Spirit permission to intervene in each person's life. Pray for each one to experience the Good News of Jesus Christ more deeply. Conclude with a prayer like the Our Father or the Hail Mary.

Part Two
Recognizing God's Invitation to Others

St. Frances Cabrini described the "holy madness" that compels us to offer evangelizing invitations when she said, "This will be the main purpose of all my interests and all that comes my way as work: to love Jesus, to seek Jesus, to speak of Jesus, and to make Jesus known." For her, this meant putting aside a serious heart condition and entering the coal mines of Colorado to teach men about God on their lunch breaks. For our friend Imogene, it means using contemporary Christian hymns with her English as a Second Language class and then inviting her students to parish prayer services where they can sing these hymns. For a professor named Jack at Holy Cross College, it meant inviting John to a retreat. In this chapter's opening mini-witness, it meant inviting people to a daily televised Mass in a nursing home room.

In the words of Pope St. John Paul II, following Jesus "involves living as he lived, accepting his message, adopting his way of thinking, embracing his destiny and sharing his project, which is the plan of the Father: it involves inviting everyone to communion with the Trinity and to communion among ourselves in a just and fraternal society." He added, "The burning desire to invite others to encounter the One whom we have encountered is the start of the evangelizing mission to which the whole Church is called."[38] All of the people in the examples above were followers of Jesus, intentional disciples who had a burning desire to invite others to encounter Jesus.

We first learned about inviting people into a faith community from Fr. Cyril. We were part of a small Christian community that staffed a religious education program in an inner-city parish. One week there were only four children who showed up for our catechetical sessions. Fr. Cyril noticed right away. Then he came over to the two of us and said, "You stand right here. I will go get you some more children and families to come." And he did just that! His positive, confident attitude and the fruits of his efforts gave us hope that we could do the same thing.

Invitations to Communal Faith

But how can you share explicit invitations to experience faith among the members of your parish? How can you become more like St. John the Baptist, who pointed out Jesus to others? The answer is this: whatever gatherings give you the strength to live the Christian life are worth inviting someone else to enjoy.

Our friend Jim offers an example of an evangelizing invitation. Jim was attending a Catholic conference in Houston, Texas, that was interrupted by Tropical Storm Allison and catastrophic flooding. The whole downtown tunnel system was inundated with water. Just a few downtown streets were dry, so Jim carefully made his way to the convention center along with a fraction of the registered participants. As he approached the corner of the building, he noticed a man standing across the street by himself, so he took a few minutes to talk with him. Larry had come to the convention hall for a gun show that had been cancelled. So Jim invited him to come to the Catholic conference for a few minutes. That few minutes turned into several hours as they shared their stories and concerns. Larry and Jim even joined a caravan of small vehicles and buses when the conference was relocated to a church on the opposite side of the city. When these two new friends said good-bye at the end of the day, Larry thanked Jim and told him that he felt as if he didn't need to buy a gun after spending the day praying with everybody.

Jim and Larry's story reminds us of an important reason why we invite others to join us in our faith communities. God loves us just the way we are, but God loves us too much to leave us the way we are, especially when we are alone and lost by the side of the road to heaven.

Invitations to Small Communities of Faith

When we talk about evangelizing invitations, we are talking about several layers of invitations. First and foremost is the invitation to a personal and deepening relationship with the Father, Son, and Holy Spirit, as aided by the faith community. The second layer of invitations is to a relationship with the body of Christ on many levels and in many settings: small communities, large gatherings, and liturgies. Any one of these settings might be a good beginning for someone. Ask God which one might be most comfortable for the person with whom you have been sharing: a small faith-sharing group, a larger parish-wide event, a social gathering, or a liturgy. Any one of them can become a door into the life of the parish community.

For a person who needs nurturing in the Christian life, a good choice is often a gathering of a small faith community—a Bible study, a workshop and meal combination, a retreat, or even a seasonal parish event. Keep in mind that the more outgoing the group is and the more the members actively seek visitors and new members, the more successful the group will be as an entry point into the parish faith community. In short, the gift of hospitality must be active and evident in the life of the group.

Some good questions to ask the members of a small faith community that is stuck and not generating new members are these: Do we as a group pay particular attention to inactive believers and the unchurched? Would they feel comfortable with us? Would we welcome them in God's name? Would they feel like strangers? Is one of our goals to guide newcomers to the pew or the folding chair, where they might experience faith as the gift behind all gifts and God's love behind all loves? All of our small groups, and even our ministry groups, must be reexamined for their potential to connect inactive believers and unchurched people with Jesus Christ in our midst.

Suggested Invitations

"The present time is . . . marked by a formidable challenge to undertake a 'new evangelization,' a proclamation of the Gospel which is always new and always the bearer of new things, an evangelization which must be 'new in its ardor, methods, and expression,'" Pope John Paul II wrote (*Veritatis Splendor*, 106). Inviting people into the community of faith may require you to think of something new and outside the box, something inspired by the Holy Spirit that draws people to Christ.

So be creative about the form that your invitations take. Ask the saints to help you take this fourth step in sharing your faith. You can invite people during a conversation or through a printed card, a website, or social media. More than one person can offer invitations to the same gatherings. Such invitations might also include supplying the means that are necessary for the person to be able to come, such as transportation or babysitting. It also entails warmly greeting people when they arrive for events.

Below is a list of invitations that you might consider sharing with someone. When someone accepts your invitation to a small group, a parish event, a liturgy, or a social gathering, be sure to ask them afterward, "What was the experience like for you?" Then listen to your guest's observations and questions. Avoid asking, "Did you like it?" Open-ended conversations can bring your relationship to a new and deeper level and open the door for other members of the community of faith to interact with your guest during future visits.

- Invite inactive or marginal Catholics to go with you to Christmas or Easter Mass.
- Invite a friend or neighbor to a parish picnic, carnival, supper, dance, beach party, etc.
- Invite someone to go with you on a pilgrimage to a recognized Catholic shrine.
- Invite someone to a retreat, Cursillo, healing Mass, Marriage Encounter weekend, or prayer group.
- Invite a friend or neighbor to a meeting of your small faith-sharing group that includes a time for socializing.
- Invite someone for dinner along with several members of your parish.

- Bring someone to a parish or diocesan adult religious education course or workshop like the *Catholicism* series by Rev. Robert Barron listed in the resource section or his newer series entitled *Catholicism: The New Evangelization.*
- Start a parish summertime arts or movie program.
- Start a walking club or exercise class in your parish and invite a friend to come along.
- Encourage your parish to have a Christian concert or play and bring someone with you to the performance.
- Consider a short-term evangelization project like a Christmas Carol Festival, which includes parish-wide invitations, carol singing, witnesses, prayer, and refreshment. (Visit www.christmascarolfestival.com for more information.)
- Invite young adults to serve food or cook for a soup kitchen or participate in a Habitat for Humanity project, a literacy volunteer effort, or a community initiative like transplanting trees.

This last suggestion is based on information about young adults (ages eighteen to thirty-five) and their natural inclinations to help those in need. Too often we assume that evangelizing invitations should be for events and liturgies that are explicitly religious, where young adults are the recipients of what we have to offer. This is only part of the story as far as young adults go. Many find direct service to be very appealing, and many want to be needed in some significant way. This means that inviting young people to serve can be a natural choice. And when the service we provide with them is done in a prayerful, compassionate, and Christ-centered way, then young adults can be drawn into the life of the faith community.

Blessed Josefa Naval Girbes (1820–1893) felt inspired to reach out to young women, so she began offering needlework and embroidery lessons for small groups. During these lessons, she also offered spiritual readings and impromptu religious discussions. While the women practiced needlepoint, she taught them basic catechism, stressing the importance of prayer and meditation and encouraging them to participate in church activities. Blessed Josefa used her gift for needlework to gather a group of women together and bring them to the light of Christ.

Spiritual Workout for Moving Forward: Stages in the Evangelization Process[39]

Your invitations into parish life can contribute to the parish evangelization process. The process has at least seven stages that are rooted in the New Testament and a variety of Church documents. These stages are listed below, along with descriptions of what the average person can do to contribute to this process. You will recognize ways of caring, sharing, and daring to offer invitations in this summary. Read the list and then answer the questions below.

1. *Befriend People.* The whole process begins with befriending others, whether it is at the doors of the church, through parish programming, or through efforts to build quality relationships. Friendship is also our aim when we serve others through works of charity and social justice.

2. *Share Faith Stories.* As we get to know someone and listen in a caring way, we might share similar ways that God has been present in our own lives or in a saint's life. Or we may affirm a step that someone has taken toward God.

3. *Retell the Christ Story.* When the time is right, we can share who Jesus Christ really is, what he has done for us, and what he wants to do for others. The Good News at the heart of the gospel message is that we are not alone. We are not orphans. When we share this news, we put flesh on the Apostle's Creed, our baptismal vows, and even the Sign of the Cross.

4. *Invite to Conversion.* When someone is unaware of Christ's presence, we can invite him or her into reflective silence (to look within), and then invite this person to pray aloud or in silence. Conversion is a lifelong journey that involves hundreds of encounters with Jesus Christ in a wide variety of circumstances.

5. *Bring into Community.* We trust that Jesus is already present to the person we are serving. We affirm the actions of the Holy Spirit. When the time is right, we invite a person into our faith community (small group, large group, or liturgy, as appropriate). If our invitation is rejected, we refocus on God's unconditional love for this brother or sister in Jesus Christ.

6. *Call to Discipleship.* We choose to live as disciples of Jesus through the witness of a Christian life, through loving others, and through faithfulness to our vocation of marriage, the single

life, or religious life. We invite others to be transformed by a relationship with Jesus and to apply gospel values at home, in the community, and in society at large.

7. *Call to Stewardship.* The fruit of discipleship is stewardship. After a person has given his or her whole life to Jesus, the next step is to act out that surrender by placing one's resources at the apostles' feet (Acts 4:32-35). One hundred percent is given to God first, and we take back only what we need in order to live and to continue the mission of Christ.

Including people in the parish is everyone's calling! Everyone's gifts are needed. Any small action in any one of these stages can provide a doorway for someone to enter or return to full participation in the parish. We are called to befriend people, to share faith stories, to tell the Christ story, to invite each person to turn to Jesus, to usher people into the faith community, to encourage discipleship, and to act as good stewards of the gospel of Christ every day and in every way we can.

Use these questions to explore your initial response to Part Two. Your reflections can be shared with a friend or in a small group setting.

1. Who in your life has invited you to believe in Jesus? Who has invited you to become part of a faith community or parish through words or actions? Which stage of the evangelization process has this person represented for you?

2. Which stage is most suitable for using the gifts you have to offer? What concrete step might you take to become a more faithful steward of your gifts in your parish?

3. Which two stages of the evangelization process in your parish are most successful in bringing people closer to Jesus and the Church? Why? What stage(s) does your parish struggle with the most? What might be done to strengthen this stage of the process?

Closing Prayer

O Jesus, [delight] of hearts, living fountain, light of intellects,
You surpass all joys and all desires.
Let all confess Jesus, let all earnestly ask for His love;
Let all zealously seek Jesus and in seeking Him become
    enkindled with love.
May our voices praise you, O Jesus;
May the whole course of our lives give testimony to You;
May our hearts love You now and forever. Amen.

—St. Bernard of Clairvaux (1090–1153)[40]

CHAPTER SIX

FOSTERING AN EVANGELIZING, MISSIONARY PARISH

Opening Prayer

We ask you, Holy Father, to send us the light of your Spirit. Instruct our hearts. Make us holy and wise, that we might share the faith that we love in the name of Christ our Lord.

Come Holy Spirit, soul of the Church. We surrender our lives, our relationships, and all the ministries of our parish through you, in Jesus, to the Father. Fill our hearts with a new and holy compassion for our missing sisters and brothers. Enkindle in us the fire and energy of your love. Then do with us as you will. Send us forth, O Holy Spirit, as re-created and renewed disciples of Jesus the Christ. Amen.

Opening Scripture

"I am the true vine, and my Father is the vine-grower. He removes every branch in me that bears no fruit. Every branch that bears fruit he prunes to make it bear more fruit. You have already been cleansed by the word that I have spoken to you. Abide in me as I abide in you. Just as the branch cannot bear fruit by itself unless it abides in the vine, neither can you unless you abide in me. I am the vine, you are the branches. . . . My Father is glorified by this, that you bear much fruit and become my disciples. As the Father has loved me, so I have loved you; abide in my love." (John 15:1-5, 8-9)

Mini-Witness: Chopped Liver?

John was invited by our pastor to offer an adult Bible study every Sunday morning during the children's religious education sessions. John and the pastor invited people on a weekly basis, and it was announced at Masses, but only a trickle of parents and visitors dribbled in during the first three months, and for the next three months only Maria came. So John reported to the pastor, "Father, I have good news and bad news. The good news is that one woman has come every week since we started. She's really growing and wants to become a Bible study leader. The bad news is—she's not from our parish!"

Two years later, Maria invited John to a Catholic Bible study that she had started in her home. When he arrived, it was hard to find a place to park. He had to walk for several blocks. As he approached the house, there were fifty to sixty people visible through the windows. He wondered, "Was there a party going on? Do I have the right house?" Then he checked the address and stopped in his tracks. He looked up to heaven and said, "God, I had only one person in my Bible study, but Maria has sixty people in her Bible study. . . . What am I, chopped liver?"

Part One
God's Invitation to Be Disciples in the Body of Christ

In the mini-witness on the previous page, perhaps John was hoping to produce a fully grown grapevine, while God knew that attaching just one branch (Maria) would take time. It was only in hindsight that God challenged him to see beyond his efforts and enjoy the fruitfulness of her efforts as part of the same vine. The opening Scripture passage uses the vine and the branches as an image for the Church, but there are so many more that can be used to help us grasp what God calls us to be as parishes—the body of Christ, the new Jerusalem, the one sheepfold, the temple of living stones, the barque (ship) of St. Peter, and the people of God. Each image illuminates a piece of the picture. How many of us are content to do what God asks in our parishes without envy or impatience? How many of us pray for the Church using a variety of images so we can get beyond the rough spots? How many of us realize that the call to evangelize—to prayer, caring, sharing faith, and offering invitations—is at the heart of our relationships within and beyond the body of Christ?

A Community on a Mission Together

"Say therefore to the Israelites, . . . 'I will redeem you with an outstretched arm and with mighty acts of judgment. I will take you as my people, and I will be your God'" (Exodus 6:6-7). This passage recalls our origin as the people of God. It is important to note that the Lord did not say, "You will be my *person* and I will be your God." It is a modern-day illusion that we can live or serve God alone; we are called and sent together. Here is what Pope St. John Paul II said in his apostolic letter *Novo Millennio Ineunte* [At the Beginning of the New Millennium]:

> A spirituality of communion indicates above all the heart's contemplation of the mystery of the Trinity dwelling in us, and whose light we must also be able to see shining on the face of the brothers and sisters around us. A spirituality of communion also means an ability to think of our brothers and sisters in faith within the profound unity of the Mystical Body, and therefore as "those who are a part of me." This makes us able to share their joys and sufferings, to sense their desires and attend to their needs, to offer them deep and genuine friendship. (43)

So we must come together often, to be renewed and recreated and sent again. We need to regroup like a family after the death or birth of one of its members. We also come together to build upon the strength of the sacraments, which are, according to the *Catechism*, "'powers that come forth' from the Body of Christ, which is ever-living and life-giving. They are actions of the Holy Spirit at work in his Body, the Church" (1116). And in the midst of our gathering, we hope that the many people who come to us for sacraments and services will find Jesus in a thousand different compassionate ways. So we pray that when we gather, there are many mini-reunions between those who have remained and those who have walked away from the Church, and we constantly seek the grace of moving beyond ourselves together. As Pope Francis has warned, "When the Church does not come out of herself to evangelize, she becomes self-referential and then gets sick," like the crippled woman in Luke's Gospel (13:10-170.[41]

Hot Meals and Hope beyond Imagining

We experienced the care of a whole faith community several years ago during one very cold January in Wisconsin, when John was the director of religious education at St. Patrick's Parish. One cloudy Wednesday, Therese rushed off to an appointment over a poorly shoveled sidewalk. She never saw the patch of ice. Slam! She landed seat first on the sidewalk and broke a bone in her lower back.

Three months of mandatory bed rest was the only remedy. As we were agonizing over Therese's plight and the needs of our four children, ages three to twelve, we heard a knock at the door. It was Marsha, with a cardboard box containing a hot supper for the six of us. But what was even more heartwarming was the sheaf of papers on top of the box. Marsha had recruited and scheduled a dozen people to bring us supper every night for the next three months. One elderly couple even came during a blizzard. Marsha had a second list with the names of women who would do housework and laundry twice a week. We cried out of relief and gratitude for this amazing sign of God's love.

This parish community reflected the love of Jesus and the words of Pope Paul VI: "They radiate in an altogether simple and unaffected way their faith in values that go beyond current values, and their hope in something that is not seen and that one would not dare to imagine" (*Evangelii Nuntiando*, 21). Their actions evangelized us to deeper levels of faith in Jesus than we had ever experienced. Their care was more than just one person, plus another person, plus one more, reaching out to us. It was the act of the whole faith community.

Orchestrating Gifts and Seeing Past Faults

We can also grow in a spirituality of communion by realizing that our relationships are meant to draw strength from the love of the Trinity. Again, quoting from John Paul II's *Novo Millennio Ineunte:*

> A spirituality of communion implies also the ability to see what is positive in others, to welcome it and prize it as a gift from God: not only as a gift for the brother or sister who has received it directly, but also as a "gift for me." A spirituality of communion means, finally, to know how to "make room" for our brothers and sisters, bearing "each other's burdens" (Galatians 6:2) and resisting the selfish temptations which constantly beset us and provoke competition, careerism, distrust and jealousy. Let us have no illusions: unless we follow this spiritual path, external structures of communion will serve very little purpose. They would become mechanisms without a soul, "masks" of communion rather than its means of expression and growth. (43)

To make a difference in our secularized culture, every parish group, committee, organization, and ministry is challenged to move away from being just a collection of individuals doing good deeds or serving others. We are called as brothers and sisters who live as missionaries. We are called to make deliberate decisions to become evangelizing ministerial communities—marked by evangelizing prayer, compassionate caring, the sharing of our faith, and our daring to offer invitations to faith—ready, willing, and equipped to make disciples of Jesus. We are called to become a beacon of Christ's light both for each other and for all the people who live within the boundaries of the parish community. And this happens by grace because, as it has often been said, "The church is a hospital for sinners, not a museum for saints."

In other words, both the parish as a whole and each subgroup of the parish are called to the New Evangelization as a way of life, born of the love and forgiveness of Jesus Christ that we embrace together. "God sent his Son as Redeemer and Savior. In his Son and through him, he invites [us] to become, in the Holy Spirit, his adopted children and thus heirs of his blessed life" (*Catechism*, 1). We are sent by the Holy Spirit on a mission, the primary mission of the Church. As the U.S. bishops have said, evangelization is "the reason for the parish's existence and the objective of every ministry in the parish" (*Go and Make Disciples*, 85).

Spiritual Workout for Growth in Parish Evangelization: What's Really Working?

John's Gospel ends with this statement: "There are also many other things that Jesus did; if every one of them were written down, I suppose that the world itself could not contain the books that would be written" (21:25). That is also true now. Many of us have been evangelized or have seen others evangelized through programs and movements at work in the Catholic Church today. So consider the ways that God is already working in your parish.

Circle those things that have brought you to deeper faith in Jesus Christ and a greater sense of belonging in the Church. Draw a square around those things that have deepened the faith of someone that you know.

1. Small faith-sharing communities (where meeting together is usually an ongoing reality).

2. The Rite of Christian Initiation of Adults (RCIA).

3. Family-centered or intergenerational parish religious education programs.

4. Adult faith formation programs like *Why Catholic?* or various seasonal, short-term Bible studies.

5. Works of mercy and social justice outreach (St. Vincent de Paul, pro-life efforts, etc.).

6. Spiritual renewal movements (such as Catholic Charismatic Renewal, Cursillo, Divine Mercy, Marriage Encounter, Marian Renewal).

7. Retreats (at spiritual centers or in the parish).

8. Ministry meetings and formation events for those in parish ministry.

9. Sunday liturgies or daily Mass.

Use these questions to explore your initial response to Part One. Your reflections can be shared with a friend or in a small group setting.

1. How has one of the programs, ministries, or liturgies listed above deepened your faith in Jesus Christ and your sense of belonging in the Church? Which of the above would you like to know more about? Who could you ask about these programs in your parish or diocese?

2. How has one of the above deepened the Catholic faith of someone you know?

3. How has your membership in a small faith-sharing community, Bible study, or parish ministry brought you closer to God? What kinds of ministry meetings and activities have been helpful to your faith? How could your group be more evangelistic?

4. How is the mission of the New Evangelization already lived out in your parish? Of the items mentioned above, which one seems most successful in bringing people to encounter

Jesus Christ? How could the parish and all of its structures and groups become more evangelistic?

Part Two
Gifted by God to Evangelize Together

We have been offering evangelization training for Catholics from average and less-than-perfect parishes for many years. Inevitably, they ask a very important question: "How can I bring this vision into my parish?" Here is what we tell them. First, do what you can as a member of your parish. Second, pray for your parish. Third, look at your parish through the lens of evangelization. Finally, if you belong to a parish ministry, encourage the group to transform the way you spend your meeting times together.

Do What You Can

First, do what you can do, not what you can't! Here is an example of doing what you can. A few years ago, our parish worship space was completely remodeled, with new pews, new paint, new rugs, and new varnish. Therese took one step into the building and had an asthma attack from the outgassing of the new materials. We knew this meant that it would be several months before we could return. In the meantime, we would be "respiratory refugees." As Therese stood in the vestibule dealing with her asthma and her disappointment, an usher approached to ask if she were okay. After she explained her plight, his response was, "I am so sorry this is happening to you. I will pray for you every Sunday and watch for your return." He did what he could, and his prayerful kindness made all the difference.

God will guide you as you concentrate on what is needed in order to humbly offer prayer, Christ-centered caring, sharing of faith stories, and invitations to help others live the gospel. For example, you can practice hospitality by moving away from the end of the pew so that others can join you. You can greet people nearby and ask them their names. Then, after a few weeks, ask them, by name, how they are doing.

When our first grandchild was baptized in a parish in another state, the greeters at the church had lists in hand and were mostly focused on crowd control. Instead of saying, "Hello," they greeted us with "Last name?" We were very disappointed! So when it came time for our second grandchild to be baptized in the same parish several years later, we arrived forty minutes early and stood outside near the doors. Our greeting was "Oh, what a beautiful baby! We are so glad you brought your child to be baptized today!"

Pray for Your Parish

"Christian tradition has summarized the attitude we should adopt towards the Holy Spirit in just one idea—docility," wrote St. Josemaría Escrivá (1902–1975). "That means we should be aware of the work of the Holy Spirit all around us, and in our own selves we should recognize the gifts he distributes, the movements and institutions he inspires, the affections and decisions he provokes in our hearts."[42]

One way to be docile to the Spirit is to admit your helplessness in moving evangelization forward without the intervention and inspiration of those in positions of power. Some of us must also admit that the only thing we can do for our parish is to pray. But in any circumstance, we can still ask Jesus to show us one other person in the parish who is burning with zeal to share their faith and to gather the scattered people of God. Then together you can look for more people. Then you can call together all those who want to evangelize and invite them to pray together for your parish on a regular basis. It might be once a week in silence before the altar, but that is enough. The Holy Spirit will listen. Things will happen.

Keep in mind that God's desires are bigger than yours and envelop many believers. So avoid defining God's plan or looking for any new breakthrough in your parish, which may be hard to pinpoint. Be steadfast in your conviction that "the transmission of the faith is never an individual, isolated undertaking, but a communal, ecclesial event" (*Lineamenta*, 2). So decide to be even just a small part of gathering together the scattered people of God, thus fulfilling Isaiah's prophecy:

> Enlarge the site of your tent,
>> and let the curtains of your habitations be stretched out;
> do not hold back; lengthen your cords
>> and strengthen your stakes.
> For you will spread out to the right and to the left,
>> and your descendants will possess the nations
>> and will settle the desolate towns. (54:2-3)

Look through a Lens

Our third strategy and challenge is to use the New Evangelization as the lens for examining and transforming our personal lives, our groups, and our parishes. The process can be as simple as one individual following the suggestions in this book. For example, you could decide to arrive fifteen minutes before Mass to pray for your parish. The process of fostering an evangelizing parish might also be as comprehensive as a pastoral team reconfiguring the goals of the parish in order to make the New Evangelization *the* agenda of the parish. If we intentionally change one behavior or one of the structures that a ministry group uses, then the lens of evangelization will begin to change everything we do. And even if it takes a few years, there will be fruit. The image of the vine and the branches will come to life before your eyes as the Spirit works to grow evangelizing, missionary parishes.

When Fr. Gus came to one of our evangelization workshops, he could understand the importance of incorporating faith sharing and study into all ministry meetings because of the success he was having with parish Renew groups and Catholic Bible studies. But our suggestion that he add a faith-sharing element to large group meetings, like mandatory sessions for First Communion parents, seemed too farfetched for him at first. These parents didn't even want to be there! Still, he trusted us and decided to try it. He asked a dad who had experienced a conversion the previous year when his child received First Communion to offer a brief witness at the meeting. Fr. Gus also provided sign-up sheets for Renew groups and Bible studies that were starting in two weeks. To his surprise, over one hundred parents signed up, and he had to find ten new group leaders for them. He was very excited about what Jesus had done.

> A new evangelization is synonymous with mission, requiring the capacity to set out anew, go beyond boundaries and broaden horizons. The new evangelization is the opposite of self-sufficiency, a withdrawal into oneself, a *status quo* mentality and an idea that pastoral programs are simply to proceed as they did in the past. Today, a "business as usual" attitude can no longer be the case. (*Lineamenta*, 10)

Parish Meetings: An Encounter with Jesus[43]

The vision of parish life as a community of disciples can become the lifeblood of the parish when groups and ministries adopt a community-building format for their gatherings. If you belong to such a group or ministry, you can advocate for the following elements in your gatherings. It is best to do so with "I" statements, such as "I need to hear about Christ's presence in people's lives. It encourages me and helps me stay committed to this group." Or "I need to pray with everybody here so that I have a sense that what we are doing is flowing from God's presence."

Here are the steps for restructuring all committee, group, staff, organizational, and ministry meetings to foster shared discipleship. The goal is to rework each group's priorities in the light of the New Evangelization. When we do so, every parish meeting becomes an opportunity to encounter Jesus Christ, to build a community of disciples, and to empower each other to evangelize. The following structure for parish meetings can help you keep evangelization as the "priority of priorities." The format that we suggest, which is based on a meeting that lasts an hour and a half, has four parts: (1) prayer; (2) study; (3) sharing; and (4) business.

Prayer (5 to 10 minutes). Prayer is always first, because it is in and for Jesus Christ that our group exists. We must be willing to understand and be aware of the Lord's presence. He has promised to be among us as we serve him and one another. Plan what kind of prayer will be used ahead of time. You might use the *lectio divina* exercise on pages 58–60.

Study (10 minutes). The second component is study or learning. Ten minutes can be used to read or listen to Scripture (with a commentary), a church document, an article, or a short chapter from a book. Or you might view an online video or have someone present a short teaching about some aspect of your ministry. Study is the bridge between prayer and the faith sharing that follows. We are called to become a fruitful community "of one heart and soul" centered in Jesus Christ (Acts 4:32). Learning puts everyone on a common footing as brothers and sisters in faith.

Faith Sharing (10 to 15 minutes). A third component is sharing faith stories. Designating time for sharing also helps us build a community of brothers and sisters, not just a task-oriented group. Faith-sharing questions may arise out of the prayer and study or out of the human issues underlying the business at hand.

Business (60 minutes). A fourth component of a parish ministry or committee meeting is, of course, the business at hand: the reports, the finances, the programs, the problems that need to be solved, and envisioning and planning for the future. If we have joined as one people in Jesus Christ through prayer, study, and faith sharing, we still have an hour of productive time left for business.

These components, coupled with respectful confidentiality, bring us closer to accomplishing God's will with love and compassion. The Father, Son, and Holy Spirit come to us as a community of loving persons in the Trinity. Theirs is the new life that we are invited to embrace together in the New Evangelization.

A parish's baptism ministry group decided to use this format, mostly because they wanted to get past a deadlock over a new approach to offering parent sessions. Praying together and sharing faith stories was new and felt awkward at first, but they persisted. Then one Thursday night as they shared about a passage from the Gospel of Matthew, a woman named Pam burst into tears when someone repeated the line "Leave your gift there before the altar and go; first be reconciled to your brother" (5:24). It seems that Pam's husband had asked for a divorce, and she was despondent about their failures at reconciliation. No one in the group even knew about her situation, but everyone stopped and prayed for her. This was the beginning of new levels of mutual support that made working together much more meaningful and efficient. The deadlock melted away shortly after this group encounter with the compassion of Jesus.

Spiritual Workout for Moving Forward: The Challenges in Parish Evangelization

Parishes face some daunting challenges in their evangelization efforts. Some of these are rooted in personal difficulties. Others involve pastoral obstacles. Perhaps the biggest challenge is presented by the world around us. Pope Benedict XVI reminded us of this:

> People don't know God, they don't know Christ. A new paganism is present, and it is not enough to maintain the community of believers, although this is important. I believe that together we must find new ways of bringing the gospel to today's world by preaching Christ anew and by establishing the faith.[44]

Below is a list of some challenges or obstacles to the New Evangelization that many parishes face. After you read them, circle the three most difficult challenges or obstacles that you encounter in parish life. Cross out any statement that does not seem to be an obstacle in your parish.

1. We do not believe in the value or need for evangelization.

2. We do not know how to evangelize or haven't learned the skills to do it effectively.

3. We have experienced failure and discouragement in trying to evangelize in the past, so we stopped trying.

4. We are afraid of the cost of evangelization (time, planning, personnel, and money), or all of our resources are already tied up with other important ministries.

5. We are focused only on dealing with present issues in our parish, not on planning for future growth.

6. We use the same evangelization programs and methods that worked ten, twenty, or thirty years ago, whether they are working today or not.

7. We don't need new people in our church. We are comfortable the way we are.

8. We are afraid that if we evangelize, Jesus will send us some people that look, talk, and live differently than we do.

9. We don't have the time to deal with all the problems that new people will bring to the church.

10. We only want people in our church who come every Sunday and give generously to support the work we do.

11. Our bishop, pastors, and staff are stretched too thin trying to maintain the Church. We don't want to overburden them with the work of evangelizing.

12. We are too weak, sinful, poor, angry, depressed, emotionally deprived, or ill to evangelize others.

13. Our church leaders don't want to change their approach to ministry or delegate evangelization to others with new ideas.

14. We lack the kind of dynamic relationships with God the Father through Jesus Christ and the power of the Holy Spirit that evangelization requires.

Use these questions to explore your initial response to Part Two. Your reflections can be shared with a friend or in a small group setting.

1. Which two or three of the statements above did you cross out because they are not challenges or obstacles that you face to evangelization? Why?

2. What are three of the most difficult challenges or obstacles to evangelization that you face at the parish or diocesan level? Why?

3. How do you see God at work in one of these difficulties? What is one step you could take in dealing with one of these difficult obstacles?

4. In a message for youth in preparation for the 2005 World Youth Day in Cologne, Germany, Pope John Paul II said,

The Church needs genuine witnesses for the new evangelization: with men and women whose lives have been transformed by meeting Jesus, men and women who are capable of communicating this experience to others. The Church needs saints. All are called to holiness, and holy people alone can renew humanity.[45]

What connection do you see between dealing with these challenges and seeking holiness? How would seeking holiness make a difference in facing one of these obstacles?

Closing Prayer

Response: *Lord, strengthen us and send us forth.*

Link by link, the blessed chain
One Body in Christ—He the head, we the members. **R**

One Spirit diffused thru' the Holy Spirit in us all
One Hope—Him in heaven and eternity. **R**

One Faith—by his Word and his Church.
One Baptism and participation of his sacraments. **R**

Our Father, we his children—He above all, through all and in all.
Oh, my soul, be fastened link by link, strong as death. **R**

—Adapted from a prayer by St. Elizabeth Seton (1774–1821)[46]

FACING EMPTY PEWS AND

A BROKEN WORLD

Mini-Witness:
A Facebook Wake and a Family Funeral

When we got the call that Therese's brother Robert had died a few days after Christmas, she knew that she would begin to experience God's comfort by putting together a simple video of his life. It was how she had grieved when her dad had died eight years earlier. So she began her good-byes with her eyes and her heart. Therese combined some favorite movie clips of her brother's life and a dozen or more photos. Watching the video and listening to hymns was just what she needed to do until we could leave for the funeral.

But what about reaching out to all of her sisters, relatives, and friends who were spread out across the country? She decided to share her video on Facebook, along with a brief written eulogy. What a blessing! So many people left comments expressing their sympathy and concern that it felt like we had a little mini-wake right on Facebook.

Then we left for home for Robert's wake. It would be a simple prayer service led by a priest at the funeral parlor, with no additional speakers. Yet when Father was finished, Robert's wife, Gail, called out in a small voice, "Therese, please say something."

Gail wanted Therese's online eulogy repeated in person. What an opportunity for Therese to share God's encouragement with her family!

We have shared all of our mini-witnesses in the hope that you can begin to see the New Evangelization as a doable part of everyday life, with all of its glories and pitfalls. We share because we believe that you, too, will find unique ways to evangelize as you go. And we know that you can connect others to Jesus through evangelizing prayer, compassionate caring, words that reveal the story of salvation, and the offering of invitations into faith communities.

We pray that you will see each opportunity to give away your faith as a privilege, as an act that is part of God's plan. And we pray that as you give your faith away, it will deepen. So we repeat God's particular call through Pope Benedict XVI to you to evangelize: "The proclamation of and witness to the Gospel are the first service that Christians can render to every person and to the entire human race, called as they are to communicate to all God's love, which was fully manifested in Jesus Christ, the one Redeemer of the world."[47]

Go and Make Disciples

The U.S. bishops' landmark document *Go and Make Disciples: A National Plan and Strategy for Catholic Evangelization in the United States* gives us three goals that we can use both as a summary of what we are called to do together and as a way of evaluating individual efforts in sharing the faith that we love.

You may find that one of these goals is echoed in your life, while others need even more ongoing effort. We will paraphrase the three goals:

1. To encourage (and live) an active, enthusiastic faith in God that includes a willingness to share what God has done for each of us. To rely on God for the zeal, the words, and the Good News.

2. To invite people of every kind of spiritual belief to join us in a personal and communal love for Jesus Christ, our Savior and Lord, in the Catholic Church.

3. To foster the transformation of our world and our culture, with all of its institutions and social groupings, by bringing the light of the Good News to every human situation, and to act in ways that promote the dignity of every human person, the common good, and stewardship over all creation. The *Lineamenta* document and the U.S. bishops' document *Disciples Called to Witness* mention a few specific problems in this regard, including individualism, secularism (omission of God in a culture), materialism, and problems with collective conscience.

Pope Francis speaks about the roots of this last goal of transformation by asking,

When you give alms, do you touch the hand of the person you are giving them to or do you toss the coin at him or her? This is the problem: the flesh of Christ, touching the flesh of Christ, taking upon ourselves this suffering for the poor. . . . A poor Church for the poor begins by reaching out to the flesh of Christ. If we reach out to the flesh of Christ, we begin to understand something, to understand what this poverty, the Lord's poverty, actually is.[48]

When we pursue these three goals together, we are acting out of God's love for all humanity in word and in deed. And we are responding to humanity's deepest need. Pope St. John Paul II said, "Every person has the right to hear the 'Good News' of the God who reveals and gives himself in Christ, so that each one can live out in its fullness his or her proper calling" (*Redemptoris Missio*, 46). After quoting John Paul II, the Vatican's Congregation for the Doctrine of the Faith, in its document *Doctrinal Notes on Some Aspects of Evangelization*, adds, "It is a right which the Lord himself confers on every person, so that every man and woman is able truly to say with Saint Paul: Jesus Christ 'loved me and gave himself up for me' (Galatians 2:20). This right implies the corresponding duty to evangelize" (2).

Choose to Live as a Joyful Disciple

Pope Paul VI urges us forward:

May the world of our time, which is searching, sometimes with anguish, sometimes with hope, be enabled to receive the Good News not from evangelizers who are dejected, discouraged, impatient or anxious, but from ministers of the Gospel whose lives glow with fervor, who have first received the joy of Christ, and who are willing to risk their lives so that the kingdom may be proclaimed and the Church established in the midst of the world. (*Evangelii Nuntiandi*, 80)

How do we become such disciples? Putting this challenge into practice sometimes means focusing on just one discipline of the Christian life at a time. Here are some suggestions for choosing the life of a faith-sharing disciple. You might want to concentrate on one for a short time, or re-read the list again when you get stuck.

1. *Keep your eyes on Jesus, who is always with us.* Caught in a storm at sea, the apostles' boat was being battered by the waves when "[Jesus] came walking toward them on the sea. . . . They were terrified, saying, 'It is a ghost!' And they cried out in fear. But immediately Jesus spoke to them and said, 'Take heart, it is I; do not be afraid'" (Matthew 14:25-27).

2. *Rejoice and thank God in difficult times.* Venerable Solanus Casey taught a simple way to pray when we are discouraged: "Thank God ahead of time!" he said. Thank God for the way that Jesus will bring us through this experience. In this way, we throw ourselves on the mercy of Christ.

3. *Forgive injuries and pray for those who cause them.* Sometimes leaders fail to give us direction or stop supporting our efforts to share faith, and then we feel hurt. But we have a choice to make: to wallow in our pain or to forgive. Act out forgiveness by praying for your leaders and their well-being. Recall times when you hurt others in similar ways, and repent.

Discover the wisdom behind the saying, "Where two or three are gathered together, someone always spills the milk!"

4. *Stick with the basics of the Christian life.* Make a daily decision to follow Jesus through daily private prayer and regular reception of the sacraments. Study Scripture and Church teaching each day. Seek support from a spiritual director or network with Christian friends and family, or be part of a small faith-sharing group or ministry.

5. *Examine your priorities.* Discouragement sometimes arises from temporary amnesia about our real mission as Catholic evangelizers. So we repeat St. Frances Xavier Cabrini's reminder to us: "This will be my main purpose—to love Jesus, to seek Jesus, to speak of Jesus, and to make Jesus known." Ask yourself how your actions are carrying this mission forward.

Gifted to Persevere

It doesn't take long for Catholics who want to share their faith to experience discouragement. Parish and diocesan evangelization plans seem to move at the speed of glaciers and frequently stall. Local projects might begin with fire and fervor, but over a few months or years, they seem to sputter or burn out. Also, person-to-person faith-sharing encounters can take unexpected turns or leave us confused and disappointed. Temptations to give up on evangelizing are frequent. St. Lucy Filippini, founder of the Religious Teachers Filippini (1672–1732), encouraged her teachers during hard times by telling them, "Do not become discouraged or tire of your work. Instead, continue to labor perseveringly with even greater kindness and patience. . . . Entrust the results to Him and to Him alone."[49]

So admit you are discouraged with your evangelizing efforts when you need to. Acknowledge any underlying issues like lack of self-care, sins and guilt about what you have done, or perhaps unrealistic expectations. St. Francis de Sales (1567–1622) tells us, "Have patience with all things, but chiefly have patience with yourself. Do not lose courage in considering your own imperfections but instantly set about remedying them—every day begin the task anew."

We learned a lot about moving past discouragement from our two-year-old grandson, Ed. When he was having difficulty with a toy, he would growl a bit, then lift his toy up to one of us and say, "Stuck! Need help!" Who do you turn to when what Jesus seems to be asking is more than you can handle? Do you realize that you have many sisters and brothers facing the same struggles?

> Therefore, since we are surrounded by so great a cloud of witnesses, let us also lay aside every weight and the sin that clings so closely, and let us run with perseverance the race that is set before us, looking to Jesus the pioneer and perfecter of our faith, who for the sake of the joy that was set before him endured the cross . . . so that you may not grow weary or lose heart. (Hebrews 12:1-2, 3)

The author of Hebrews invites us to run with the Good News, even when we feel as if all we can do is crawl. The image of running is also acted out through an ancient Easter tradition.

In Jerusalem, at dawn on Easter, runners sprint with torches from the empty tomb to the four corners of the city. Do we draw strength from the Easter candle—the light of Jesus Christ—ever present among us, re-energizing us again and again? Do we rely on the extraordinary power we are given in Baptism, Confirmation, and the Eucharist? What is your answer?

We urge you to say, "Yes, Lord!" Yes, I will encourage others to focus on Jesus, the Light of lights! Yes, by the grace and the power of the Holy Spirit, I will run forward to share the faith I love with others in my everyday life. Yes, I will ignite new flames in every corner of the human heart, in my home, in my workplaces, in my ministries, and in my city. Yes, I will run forward with my brothers and sisters until we join the multitudes of saints who have loved and evangelized each other into the arms of the Father, Son, and Holy Spirit. Amen!

Closing Prayer

Pour out your Spirit, so that I might be strengthened to go forth and witness to the Gospel in my everyday life through my words and actions.
In moments of hesitation, remind me:
If not me, then who will proclaim the Gospel?
If not now, then when will the Gospel be proclaimed?
If not the truth of the Gospel, then what shall I proclaim?

—"Prayer for the New Evangelization," United States Conference of Catholic Bishops[50]

Let us ask the Lord always to direct our minds and hearts to him, as living stones of the Church, so that all that we do, our whole Christian life, may be a luminous witness to his mercy and love. In this way we will make our way towards the goal of our earthly pilgrimage, towards that most beautiful sanctuary, the heavenly Jerusalem. There, there is no longer any temple: God himself and the lamb are its temple; and the light of the sun and the moon give way to the glory of the Most High. Amen.

—Pope Francis[51]

New Evangelization Workouts

More Exercises for
Sharing Your Faith

Anyone who has embarked on a program of physical fitness knows that the most important step is not necessarily deciding how much exercising you will do but committing to keep moving in some regular, measurable way. The same is true with spiritual fitness and the activity of reaching out to share our faith. It requires practice, born of a vision of sharing our faith that propels us forward, step by step, day by day. And this vision is nourished by prayer and reflection.

When God has stirred up the same passion that Jesus and his disciples experienced in the Scriptures, then it is time to keep moving. So keep going, keep studying, and regroup often to encourage one another to grow as new evangelizers.

Here are some additional exercises that you might use along the way. They are numbered according to the corresponding chapters of this book and treat the same theme. Any or all of these exercises can be used by individuals, committees, ministry groups, or faith-sharing groups.

–1–
Scrap the Word "Evangelization"?

Some would say, "Why not scrap the word 'evangelization' and call it something else? It has too much cultural baggage. People think of TV evangelists, street-corner preaching, and in-your-face, confrontational methods of sharing beliefs when they hear that word. Catholics don't understand difficult theological words like 'evangelization.' Surely we can come up with a more palatable word or phrase!" But if we give up on the word "evangelization," if we decide to use something simpler or something more user-friendly, what might we lose?

Here are some of the reasons why you might want to embrace the word "evangelization." Choose two that might motivate you to think of yourself as an evangelizer.

1. Evangelization is scriptural. Its basis comes to us from key passages of the New Testament that reveal who Jesus Christ is, what his mission is, what he has done for us, and what he will do for others. (See, for example, Matthew 28:18-19; Luke 4:43; Mark 16:15-16; 1 Corinthians 9:16.)

2. Evangelization is at the heart of Catholic Church teaching: "We wish to confirm once more that the task of evangelizing all people constitutes the essential mission of the Church" (*Evangelii Nuntiandi*, 14).

3. Evangelization is the primary mission of the laity. They "fulfill their prophetic mission by evangelization, 'that is, the proclamation of Christ by word and the testimony of life . . . in the ordinary circumstances of the world'" (*Catechism*, 905).

4. Evangelization is an ecumenical necessity. All Christians share a common commission from Christ. Evangelization gives us opportunities to dialogue about ways of proclaiming the gospel of Jesus. It has brought together many Christians (mainline Protestants, evangelicals, Pentecostals, and Catholics) and has become a bridge between the Catholic Church and other Christian churches.

5. Evangelization was called for by Pope St. John Paul II. "No believer in Christ, no institution of the Church can avoid this supreme duty: to proclaim Christ to all peoples" (*Redemptoris Missio*, 3).

6. Evangelization was the passion of many saints, including St. Francis Xavier (1506–1552), St. Jean de Brebeuf (1593–1649), and Blessed Junipero Serra (1713–1784). Reading about the hardships they endured to spread the gospel message can be a very eye-opening experience.

Use these questions to explore your response to the statements in this exercise. Your reflections can be shared with a friend or in a small group setting.

1. What was your initial response to the word "evangelization" when you first heard it? How has your understanding changed?

2. Which two of the statements in this exercise might motivate you to learn more about evangelization?

3. What are two things you have learned about evangelization from reading this book?

–2–
Reaching Out in Prayer

This exercise is for use with a group of people who are preparing for an upcoming "evangelizing" event (mission, Bible study, retreat, workshop, or special liturgy). It works best when used from four to six weeks prior to the event. For an example of an evangelizing event, visit www.christmascarolfestival.com.

A group or parish might design a "Reaching Out in Prayer" brochure or a special invitation card that can be shared at ministry meetings and Sunday Masses. Here is what the brochure might say:

Over the next few weeks, we will be conducting a special outreach to active and inactive Catholics and people without a church home. Our primary goal is to invite others into a deeper relationship with Jesus Christ and his body, the Church. One way we can learn how to do this is by inviting people to come for _____ on _____ [fill in the blank with your parish/diocesan upcoming evangelizing event].

The success of our efforts is based on one simple principle: you are invited to bring someone, even several people. A person-to-person invitation is what makes this work. Now is the time to begin praying and asking this question: "Lord Jesus, who could I invite to come with me?"

At the Mass or meeting, be sure that the prayer brochures (or invitations) plus pencils are available for all attendees, and ask everyone to take a copy and a pencil while you explain the "Reaching Out in Prayer" exercise, which you can distribute on a separate sheet of paper.

Finding the people to invite isn't really that hard. We just have to open our eyes. Here are five easy steps: Reach Nearby, Reach Up, Reach Out, Reach Forward, and Reach After.

1. *Reach Nearby*
Who is someone that you suspect you could be praying for in a special way? Such people are probably a part of your network of everyday relationships—your circle of friends, relatives, and acquaintances who are active or inactive Catholics or have no church. List the first names of three or four of them below.

I will pray each day especially for _____.

Who do you know with very pressing needs? What are his or her spiritual needs? Now add three more names.

2. *Reach Up*
We reach up to Jesus in daily prayer for each person. Ask the Holy Spirit to touch their hearts. Watch for opportunities to share God's love with each one in a practical way. Join with others in praying for the people on your list.

3. *Reach Out*

Reach out and build stronger friendships with the people on your list. By strengthening our natural relationships, we build a stronger bond of trust. We are sowing seeds of openness to a friendship with Jesus, our ultimate Friend. Through our caring, our invitations also become invitations from God.

4. *Reach Forward*

Reach into the future and plan certain days on which you will invite each person to come to the evangelizing event with you. Offer to help with obstacles to coming, such as transportation or babysitting.

5. *Reach After*

We are each encouraged to invite at least six people (or more if you'd like). Not everyone will be interested. Not everyone who is interested will be able to come. Reach after those who show interest. They need your continued support and prayer. Consider how to extend additional invitations to them to join you at other parish or diocesan events in the future.

Use these questions to explore your response to the statements above. Your reflections can be shared with a friend or in a small group setting.

1. What was your experience of creating this list? What did you notice about the people you chose to include?

2. Stop and pray for the people on your list for one minute right now in silence. Ask for God's wisdom about inviting one or more of these people to your upcoming event.

3. Put your list aside and read it closely each day for a week. Commit yourself to spending five minutes a day over the next week to pray for the people on your "Reach Nearby" list.

−3−
Praying with Someone in Times of Need

In a survey showing how Christians share their faith, conducted by the Barna Research Group, "crisis prayer"—praying with another person in need—is the most common way Christians share their faith with others. Almost eight out of ten Christians reported having done so in the previous year.[52] Crises are a normal part of life. They can be negative stresses, transitions, or needs (e.g., death of a loved one, loss of a job, moving to a new home, etc.) or positive stresses, transitions, or needs (birth of a child, marriage, new job, etc.).

This is an exercise that offers practice in listening to and praying with others, both silently and aloud. It is an opportunity to grow in the ability to share faith. It works best with groups of two, or three when an odd number of people are present.

Appoint someone to facilitate the exercise, keeping people to the suggested times as much as possible. The facilitator can introduce the exercise by saying, "Today we will explore the connection between listening and praying. I will give you instructions about when to listen and when to pray as we go along." Please emphasize also the <u>importance of maintaining confidentiality</u> about what is shared in the small groups. Allow about forty-five minutes.

1. *Open with prayer.* You can pray the "Our Father," or use the prayer from chapter 3 of this book.

2. *Read the following Scripture passage:*

> Let each of you look not to your own interests, but to the interests of others. Let the same mind be in you that was in Christ Jesus,
>> who, though he was in the form of God,
>>> did not regard equality with God
>>> as something to be exploited,
>> but emptied himself,
>>> taking the form of a slave,
>>> being born in human likeness.
>> And being found in human form,
>>> he humbled himself
>>> and became obedient to the point of death—
>>> even death on a cross. (Philippians 2:4-8)

3. *Move into groups of two (and no more than three) people.* Choose people whom you don't know well, if possible. Introduce yourselves.

4. *Pray silently for the other person(s) in your group.* For example, "Lord Jesus, please give _____ (name) whatever he or she most needs right now."

5. *Allow time for each person in the group to share about each of the following statements. Offer one statement at a time, allowing the person two minutes to respond. After each two-minute period ends, offer the next statement.*

> "I grew up in . . . "
> "Some of the most loved people in my life are . . . "
> "One of my fondest memories as a child is . . . "
> "I am most happy when . . . "
> "One thing that really gets me angry is . . . "
> "Something that really makes me sad is . . . "

6. *Spend one minute in silence, with each person reflecting on how he or she would complete the following statement:*

> "Right now, I wish God would help me with . . . "

7. *Allow each person to share his or her response.*

8. *Take one minute to pray silently for the other person(s) and the particular need that was verbalized.*

9. *Spend five more minutes answering these question:* How were the two prayer times that you just experienced alike? How were they different? Why?

10. *Gather together and then say this closing prayer together, with the right and left sides of the room alternating verses.*

All: Praise the LORD!
Praise the LORD, O my soul!

Right: I will praise the LORD as long as I live;
I will sing praises to my God all my life long.

Left: Happy are those whose help is the God of Jacob,
whose hope is in the LORD their God,
who made heaven and earth,
the sea, and all that is in them;

Right: who keeps faith forever;
who executes justice for the oppressed;
who gives food to the hungry.

Left: The LORD sets the prisoners free;
the LORD opens the eyes of the blind.

Right: The LORD lifts up those who are bowed down;
the LORD loves the righteous.

Left: The LORD watches over the strangers;
he upholds the orphan and the widow,
but the way of the wicked he brings to ruin.

All: The LORD will reign forever,
your God, O Zion, for all generations.
Praise the LORD! (Psalm 146:1-2, 5-10)

After the session is over, spend some time reflecting on these questions as an individual or in small groups.

1. What was happening as you prayed for the other person the second time around? How were the two times you prayed for the other person different for you?

2. What is most meaningful about this exercise? What is most challenging?

3. What are your experiences of praying with someone in need? How will your approach be different after this exercise? What kinds of prayers might you use?

4. What did you realize or learn during this exercise about praying with someone who is experiencing a crisis? What did you notice about your sharing partner's gifts?

−4−
Sharing Our Faith Stories with Words

"Does anyone have suggestions for becoming more comfortable with sharing our faith stories with others?" asked Darlene at a recent evangelization training session. Darlene had recognized an important issue. Not knowing how to share faith stories can block us from telling others how Jesus has touched our lives. As a result, times when we might have shared our faith are missed, and regrets about that missed opportunity can further hinder us from trying to share faith stories again.

So how can we heed the U.S. bishops' suggestion to "take note of the many opportunities to support another's faith, to share faith, and to help build up Jesus' kingdom in our homes and workplaces, among our neighbors and friends" (*Go and Make Disciples*, 136)?

Below is a list of suggestions generated by Darlene's question. After you have read them, think about two that you might implement in your own life.

1. Pray and ask the Holy Spirit for guidance in recalling and sharing encounters and insights that you have experienced with God.

2. Listen to or read the faith stories of others (e.g., saints' lives, Scripture stories, or personal witnesses). Notice how the focus of these stories is on what Jesus has done for them.

3. Take time to reflect on your religious experiences—times when you have known that Jesus was near (e.g., the birth of a child, death of loved one, success at work, loss of a job, etc.).

4. Write down five or six faith stories in less than one hundred words each and keep them in a journal (paper or electronic, private or online). Read over them every six months and add more stories.

5. Record your faith stories in audio or video format (each no more than two or three minutes in length). Play them back every six months. This practice will give you some idea of how you sound to others. Add more stories, or re-record one of them in light of your new insights.

6. Think about family photos, video clips, or objects from everyday life that would help you tell your faith stories in memorable and inviting ways. Connecting your story to such items might also remind you to share when you see this object again. For example, when Therese sees a walker, she remembers her grandmother visiting and blessing the "old people" in her nursing home.

7. When you realize that you have missed an opportunity to share a faith story with someone, rejoice! Thank God for this realization. It means that God is giving you an evangelizing heart! Ask Jesus to open your eyes to future opportunities to reach out in spiritual compassion.

8. Use your imagination. When you miss an opportunity, imagine what you could have said. Repeat your story aloud to yourself (when appropriate). This will make what Christ has done more real for you.

9. Practice sharing your faith stories with one other person you trust. Ask him or her for feedback on how these stories sound and what might be changed. This happens naturally in small faith-sharing groups, so join a small faith-sharing group or Bible study group, if you have not already.

10. Ask someone who does a very good job of sharing personal faith stories to be your mentor, so you can learn how to share more effectively and with greater compassion. Remember, this can also be done by way of videoconferencing or over the phone.

11. Have patience. None of us notices and uses every opportunity that comes our way to share our faith in daily life. It can take years to make progress in telling our faith stories more effectively, and that is okay.

Use these questions to explore your response to the suggestions in this exercise. Your reflections can be shared with a friend or in a small group setting.

1. Recall a faith story you have heard someone else share in everyday life or at a church event. What struck you most about that story or about the person who told it?

2. Which two or three of the suggestions for preparing faith stories have you or others you know tried? What was it like to share?

3. Which of these suggestions would you most like to try? Why?

4. Why do you think telling faith stories is important for effective Catholic evangelization?

5. What other suggestions might you offer to someone who wants to learn how to share personal faith stories?

–5–
Reading the Signs: Someone Is Thinking about Returning to the Church

As we befriend people, they share with us how they feel about their lives, what they are thinking about, and where they are going. Lorene Hanley Duquin, author, speaker, and Catholic evangelizer, notes that inactive Catholics who are considering returning to the Church often share some concrete signs or cues about returning to a faith life and to church.[53]

Below are six of these signs. As you read them, try to recall any occasions when you have heard someone share such cues.

1. *Questions*

The most common sign of an imminent conversion is questioning the identity of God, the nature of good and evil, or the meaning of life. Someone might ask, "What is my life about? Why do I do what I do? Is there any purpose in all of this?" As a parent, spouse, sibling, or friend, your role is not to restore that meaning but to help the person find meaning for himself. You can do that by active listening. Nonthreatening comments, such as "It sounds like you're really searching," will encourage the person to talk in a more open manner. You don't have to offer solutions or answers. Offer your opinion only when asked.

2. *Memories*

Someone might reminisce about Catholic school, nuns, priests, or parish activities. He or she might recall childhood devotions to Our Lady or the saints. Memories of music, incense, or a special liturgy might surface. Don't be afraid to share your own memories. If remembering takes a negative turn, don't be defensive. The person may be justified in his or her anger. Sometimes talking about a bad experience can help put it in perspective. If possible, encourage the person to distinguish between anger toward a person and toward the whole Church. It wasn't the Church that caused the pain. It was a person connected to the Church. If a person is open to praying with you, ask the Holy Spirit for healing of memories.

3. *Reading*

Many inactive Catholics read or watch their way back to the Church. It's a good idea to keep Catholic books, magazines, newspapers, CDs, DVDs, and websites or blog addresses available where family members and friends can pick them up. If there's something in particular that you think might be of interest, recommend it to family members and friends. One woman sent books on Dorothy Day and Edith Stein to her sister, who was struggling with how she perceived the treatment of women by the Church.

4. *Current Events*

Catholic news events can trigger interest in some people. Make sure you're up-to-date on papal visits, Marian apparitions, Vatican announcements, and local news about Catholic people and events. Even the sex-abuse scandal is an opportunity to share why you are still Catholic! When discussing any aspect of Catholic news, it's a good idea to emphasize the universality of the Church. Unlike many Christian denominations, the Catholic Church numbers one billion people from widely different cultural, intellectual, and socioeconomic backgrounds. As Irish writer James Joyce once said, the Catholic Church means "Here comes everybody!"

5. Major Life Events

Illness, death, divorce, the birth of a baby, a job loss or transfer, kids growing into their teenage years, moving to a new home—all these events can trigger a desire to return to the Church. Sometimes people are afraid that the Church will reject them if they have been gone for a long time. Some think they are excommunicated. You might find yourself in a position to help someone get accurate information about where they stand with God and the Church.

6. God's Presence

The real presence of Jesus Christ in the Eucharist is often a factor in bringing people back. Invite people to come with you to family funerals, weddings, baptisms, First Communions, confirmations, May crownings, and Mass on Ash Wednesday, Easter, and Christmas. It's hard for people to go to church by themselves. Be an inviter. If they don't want to go to Mass, invite them to parish social, cultural, or educational events. Keep the lines of communication open. Radiate God's love to everyone you meet. Before long, people will be attracted to the Church because they want the faith, love, and peace that you possess.

Use these questions to explore your response to the signs described in this exercise. Your reflections can be shared with a friend or in a small group setting.

1. Jot down the first names of three people from your everyday life who are not regular churchgoers. If you are sharing with a group, just use first names.

2. What do you know about each of their reasons for being inactive Catholics?

3. Have you noticed any of these six signs in any of the three people you named?

4. How might Jesus invite you to reach out to one of these people? To inactive Catholics in general?

– 6 –
The Media World of Twenty- and Thirty-Something Adults

There are many ways to share your faith in the digital world, including social media, blogs, websites, and e-mail on computers, tablets, and smartphones. Why we would do so depends on our beliefs about the value of media and our preferences in using it. For people in their twenties and thirties, the reason to be engaged with others was aptly summed up by the character of Facebook founder Mark Zuckerberg in the movie *The Social Network*: "We lived on farms, then we lived in cities, and now we're going to live on the Internet!"

For those of us who are not quite that young, we can take our cue from Pope St. John Paul II, who was at an advanced age when he said,

> Like the new frontiers of other times, [the Internet] is full of the interplay of danger and promise, and not without the sense of adventure which marked other great periods of change. For the Church the new world of cyberspace is a summons to the great adventure of using its potential to proclaim the Gospel message. This challenge is at the heart of what it means at the beginning of the millennium to follow the Lord's command to "put out into the deep" (Luke 5:4).[54]

What part do technology and social media play in your every-day life and in sharing with others? What devices do you own, and how do you use them? What is it like for you to share what is meaningful to you on the Internet? Estimate how often you participate in the following activities and your attitude about communicating with each one. Put a "D" for daily, a "W" for weekly, or an "N" for never. Then, from 1 to 5, rate how comfortable you are with using that technology, with "1" being very comfortable to "5" being very uncomfortable.

_____E-mail

_____Texting

_____Surfing the Internet

_____Facebook

_____Twitter

_____Podcasts

_____Cell phone

_____Smartphone

_____Smartphone apps

_____Online chat

_____E-books

_____Online video viewing

_____Videoconferencing

_____Online purchases

_____Blog writing or reading

Use these questions to explore your response to the survey above. Your reflections can be shared with a friend or in a small group setting.

1. In today's world, we have many options for communicating with one another across time and space. Which is your preferred means of communication—telephone, letter writing, e-mail, texting, social networking sites, or online chats? Why is this your preferred method?

2. What is the preferred method for young adults, friends, or family members with whom you have regular contact?

3. What methods listed above are used in your parish? How are they working?

4. What is one step you could take to be more comfortable with one of these activities for the sake of your personal relationships or to build your parish community?

-7-

The Christ Story in China

The following is an example of one of the many ways to share the Good News about Jesus. Fr. Eugene LaVerdiere, SSS, told this story at Assumption College in Worcester, Massachusetts, during the 1994 Summer Ecumenical Institute. The whole session was called "Gospel Stories and Our Stories."

Note that this example is related to material in the first chapter, "Burning with Zeal." Fr. LaVerdiere concentrates on just one part of the gospel message, the "S" for the Savior that we have in Jesus. And he begins with just one of the titles of Jesus, one that a person from an Eastern religion could easily understand. He leaves the rest of the story for a local priest to tell.

Fr. Eugene fulfilled a lifelong dream when he visited China and the coastal island where St. Francis Xavier died. One day during his trip, while in a town on the mainland, he decided to take a walk along the Lee River. He was surprised when a young man of sixteen stopped him.

"Excuse me, what is your nationality?" the young man asked. Then he asked about the city Fr. Eugene had come from. After Father's reply, the young man asked if he could walk with him and practice speaking his English.

"What is your profession in America?" was the teen's next question.

Father answered, "I am a Catholic priest."

"Oh, yes," the young man responded. "Catholics are the ones who go like this," and he made the Sign of the Cross. "I saw tourists do it in a restaurant, and they said they did this because they were Catholic."

"Do you know what it means?" asked the priest.

"No," said the young man.

"Let me explain. A long, long time ago, when China was still a young country, not much more than two hundred years old, there lived a very great teacher. His name was Jesus. He lived way on the other side of Asia. And everyone was coming to hear him from many places because they knew there was something very special about this man. He healed the sick and did many miracles. He called God his father and said he was his son. Little by little, people began to recognize that he was really God's Son, and because of that, he loved everyone. We all know that it is very hard to love every single person. And it is even harder to accept someone who thinks that every person is to be loved. So little by little, people found a way to have him put to death on a cross.

"We Catholics don't love everybody very well, but we would really like to. So we remind ourselves of Jesus by making on our very own person the sign of the cross on which he died."

The young man was so impressed that he volunteered to help Fr. LaVerdiere buy a ticket for a bus ride for the following morning, saving the priest an expensive taxi fare. The next day, the young man was at the bus station an hour and a half early with a small meal. In return, Father gave the young man the name of a local Catholic man. "If you want to know more about this great teacher, you can go to this man. He knows a lot about him."

Use these questions to explore your response to this story. Your reflections can be shared with a friend or in a small group setting.

1. How has your idea of being on a mission changed since you began studying how to share your faith in everyday life? Under what circumstances would you call yourself an evangelizer or a missionary?

2. Think of the young man in the story, who had seen a tourist pray the Sign of the Cross in a restaurant. What would it mean for you to share faith in some public way? What might this kind of sharing look like in your own life?

3. How would you retell the Christ story in your own words? Under what circumstances would you do so? What part do you see yourself playing in bringing the gospel to all the nations?

GLOSSARY OF TERMS

Charisms:[55] Free gifts of grace given by the Holy Spirit that enable us to undertake various tasks for the evangelization, renewal, and building of the Church. It is important to keep in mind that the Holy Spirit is the gift, and individual charisms are meant to be manifestations of the Spirit's activity. See a list of charisms in 1 Corinthians 12:4-11, Romans 12:3-8, 1 Peter 4:10-11, and Ephesians 4:1-16, as well as in references in the *Catechism of the Catholic Church* (799, 800).

Conversion: A change of heart, a spiritual transformation experienced by an individual. It is a movement toward God in Jesus Christ that comes about through the power of the Holy Spirit. Conversion involves a continuous process that occurs in the emotional, intellectual, moral, and social areas of our lives.

Evangelization: In *Evangelii Nuntiandi,* Pope Paul VI says, "Evangelizing means bringing the Good News into all the strata of humanity, and through its influence transforming humanity from within and making it new" (18). Evangelization includes proclaiming Jesus in word or deed, plus the response of the person who accepts Jesus through the activity of the Holy Spirit.

Faith Sharing: In this book, we are making a distinction between faith sharing and sharing your faith. **Faith sharing** is a mutual exchange about one's relationship with Jesus Christ and is usually experienced in the context of a small group or with a spiritual friend. Both people have a spoken or unspoken agreement to share in this way. **Sharing your faith** is a much broader term that includes intercessory prayer, acts of caring, sharing a faith story, and inviting others to Jesus and the Church. It happens when a person of faith decides to bring a spiritual dimension into a relationship for the sake of another. It is an act of evangelization.

Faith Story: The retelling of an event in one's life that has spiritual significance because you experienced Jesus Christ as a living person, realized a call to a deeper faith, or became more aware of God's personal love. The purpose of doing so is to glorify God and to give others hope about God's presence. The event's meaning is also explained within the context of one's ongoing relationship with God.

Inactive Catholic: Someone who identifies himself or herself as Catholic but goes to Sunday liturgies less than twice in six months, not counting Christmas, Easter, weddings, and funerals. For many who identify themselves as "Catholic," the term is just one of many descriptors they would use for themselves, similar to "Italian," "single," or "college graduate."

Lineamenta: A document written in preparation for the Ordinary General Assembly of the Synod of Bishops on the New Evangelization for the Transmission of the Christian Faith. The Synod met at the Vatican in October 2012. For a summary of what was discussed at this meeting, visit http://www.zenit.org/en/articles/official-summary-of-the-final-message-of-the-synod-of-bishops.

New Evangelization: Renewed efforts to engage persons, communities, and nations in our changing world with the Good News of Jesus Christ. Efforts are usually geared at reaching active, inactive, marginal, and unchurched Catholics, as well as others with no church affiliation. At the present time, the Church is directing the focus of the New Evangelization to persons and Christian communities who may have received sacraments but are primarily inactive or unchurched.

Proselytize: To persuade someone to switch religions, usually by any means necessary.

Unchurched: Someone who does not identify with any church. It is defined by the Gallup polling organization as those who answer no to either one or both of the following questions: "Do you happen to be a member of a church, synagogue, or mosque?" and "Apart from weddings, funerals, or special holidays, such as Christmas, Easter or Yom Kippur, have you attended the church, synagogue, or mosque of your choice in the past six months, or not?"[56]

Witness: To give credibility to what you believe by living a life that reflects God's love and/or to engage in explicit conversations that include sharing faith stories or a brief summary of what Jesus means in the context of your whole life.

Recommended Resources

Our websites, www.johnandthereseboucher.com and www.catholicevangelizer.com, provide resources for evangelizing in families, parishes, and beyond. Here are other resources that you might find helpful.

Archdiocese of Louisville. *Christian Hospitality: A Handbook for Parishes* (pamphlet). Louisville, KY: Archdiocese of Louisville, 2013. http://www.archlou.org/archlou/acc.

Barron, Robert. *Catholicism Study Program: Journey Deep into the Faith*. Skokie, IL: Word on Fire Ministries.

Boguslawski, Steven, OP, and Ralph Martin, eds. *The New Evangelization: Overcoming the Obstacles*. Mahwah, NJ: Paulist Press, 2008.

Boucher, John and Therese. *Praying for Our Adult Sons and Daughters: Placing Them in the Heart of God*. Frederick, MD: The Word Among Us Press, 2012.

Catechism of the Catholic Church: Second Edition. New York: Doubleday Religion, 2003. Sections on Evangelization, Missions, Gospel, Jesus, and Holy Spirit.

Committee on Evangelization and Catechesis. *Disciples Called to Witness: The New Evangelization*. Washington, DC: United States Conference of Catholic Bishops, Inc., 2012.

Congregation for the Doctrine of the Faith. *Doctrinal Note on Some Aspects of Evangelization.* December 14, 2007. http://www.vatican.va/roman_curia/congregations/cfaith/documents/rc_con_cfaith_doc_20071203_nota-evangelizzazione_en.html.

DeSiano, Frank, CSP, and Kenneth Boyack, CSP. *Discovering My Experience of God: Awareness and Witness.* Mahwah, NJ: Paulist Press, 1992.

————. *Perspectives for the Synod on the New Evangelization: A View from the United States.* Washington, DC: Paulist Evangelization Ministries, 2012.

Duquin, Lorene Hanley. "Fishing with Nets and Fishing with Poles: Reaching Inactive and Alienated Catholics." Paulist National Catholic Evangelization Association's Catholic Speakers Online Presentation, June 5, 2008. Adobe Flash file, 58:17. http://www.pemdc.org/events/cso-duquin.aspx.

————. *When a Loved One Leaves the Church: What You Can Do.* Huntington, IN: Our Sunday Visitor, 2001.

Gray, Mark M., Ph.D, and Paul M. Perl, Ph.D. *Sacraments Today: Belief and Practice Among U.S. Catholics.* Washington, DC: Center for Applied Research in the Apostolate (CARA), 2008. http://cara.georgetown.edu/sacramentsreport.pdf.

Hater, Fr. Robert J. The Parish Guide to the New Evangelization. Huntington, IN: Our Sunday Visitor, 2013.

Hayes, Mike. *Googling God: The Religious Landscape of People in Their 20s and 30s*. Mahwah, NJ: Paulist Press, 2007.

Ivereigh, Austen. *How to Defend the Faith without Raising Your Voice: Civil Responses to Catholic Hot Button Issues*. Huntington, IN: Our Sunday Visitor, 2012.

Krisak, Fr. Tony. "Are You Saved Yet?" *Evangelization Exchange*, March 2012. www.pemdc.org/ee0312-krisak/.

_____. "Longing for an Invitation." *Evangelization Exchange*, May 2011. www.pemdc.org/ee0511-krisak/.

_____. "Conversations about Faith." *Evangelization Exchange*, October 2010. www.pemdc.org/ee1010-conversations/

Paul VI. *Evangelii Nuntiandi* [On Evangelization in the Modern World]. Washington, DC: United States Conference of Catholic Bishops, 1976.

Paulist Evangelization Ministries. 3031 Fourth St., NE, Washington, DC 20017. (202) 832-5022. www.pncea.org.

Paulist Young Adult Ministries, 405 W. 59th St., New York, NY. www.BustedHalo.com. For ministry to people in their 20s and 30s.

Pew Research Center's Forum on Religion & Public Life. *Faith in Flux: Changes in Religious Affiliation in the U.S.* Washington,

DC: Pew Research Center, 2009. http://www.pewforum.org/files/2009/04/fullreport.pdf.

Synod of Bishops. *New Evangelization for the Transmission of the Christian Faith: Lineamenta.* XIII Ordinary General Assembly. 2012. http://www.vatican.va/roman_curia/synod/documents/rc_synod_doc_20110202_lineamenta-xiii-assembly_en.html.

RENEW Theology on Tap. RENEW International, 1232 George St., Plainfield, NJ 07062, 908–769–5400. renewtot@renewintl.org, www.theologyontap.com.

United States Conference of Catholic Bishops. *Go and Make Disciples: A National Plan and Strategy for Catholic Evangelization in the United States.* Washington, DC: United States Conference of Catholic Bishops, Inc., 2002.

Weddell, Sherry A. *Forming Intentional Disciples: The Path to Knowing and Following Jesus.* Huntington, IN: Our Sunday Visitor, 2012.

Wright, Allan F. *Jesus, the Evangelist: A Gospel Guide to the New Evangelization.* Cincinnati, OH: Franciscan Media, 2013.

Wuerl, Cardinal Donald. *New Evangelization: Passing on the Catholic Faith Today.* Huntington, IN: Our Sunday Visitor, 2013.

ENDNOTES

1. Mark M. Gray, Ph.D, and Paul M. Perl, Ph.D, *Sacraments Today, Belief and Practice Among U.S. Catholics* (Washington, DC: Center for Applied Research in the Apostolate [CARA], 2008), http://cara.georgetown.edu/sacramentsreport.pdf. The study also revealed that 56 percent of adult Catholics attend Mass a few times a year, rarely, or never (20).

2. Barna Research Group, "Most Americans Consider Easter a Religious Holiday, but Fewer Correctly Identify Its Meaning," Barna Research Group, March 15, 2010, https://www.barna.org/barna-update/article/13-culture/356-most-americans-consider-easter-a-religious-holiday-but-fewer-correctly-identify-its-meaning#.UkCPltJ6bJY.

3. Pew Research Center's Forum on Religion & Public Life, *U.S. Religious Landscape Survey: Religious Beliefs and Practices; Diverse and Politically Relevant* (Washington, DC: Pew Research Center, 2008), http://www.pewforum.org/files/2008/06/report2-religious-landscape-study-full.pdf.

4. Congregation for the Doctrine of the Faith, *Doctrinal Notes on Some Aspects of Evangelization,* 2007, 2, http://www.vatican.va/roman_curia/congregations/cfaith/documents/rc_con_cfaith_doc_20071203_nota-evangelizzazione_en.html.

5. Benedict XVI, "Address of His Holiness Pope Benedict XVI to the Participants of the International Conference on Occasion of the 40th Anniversary of the Conciliar Decree 'Ad Gentes,'" March 11, 2006.

6. For more information, go to http://www.pemdc.org/signup.aspx.

7. Benedict XVI, *Verbum Domini* [The Word of God in the Life and Mission of the Church], September 30, 2010, 91.

8. Anthony F. Chiffolo, *At Prayer with the Saints* (Liguori, MO: Liguori Publications, 1998), 124.

9. Brother Claude Lane, OSB, Mary, Star of Evangelization (St. Benedict, OR: Mt. Angel Abbey, 2003), http://www.archdpdx .org/icon/prayer-english.html.

10. United States Conference of Catholic Bishops, *Go and Make Disciples: A National Plan and Strategy for Catholic Evangelization in the United States* (Washington, DC: United States Conference of Catholic Bishops, Inc., 2002), 67.

11. Paul VI, *Evangelii Nuntiandi* [On Evangelization in the Modern World], December 8, 1975, 14.

12. John Paul II, *Veritatis Splendor* [The Splendor of Truth], August 6, 1993, 106.

13. John Paul II, *Redemptoris Missio* [Mission of the Redeemer], December 7, 1990, 3.

14. Cindy Wooden, "Pope Announces Formation of Pontifical Council for New Evangelization," *Catholic News Service*, June 28, 2010, http:// www.catholicnews.com/data/stories/ cns/1002665.htm.

15. "Pentecost Vigil: The Church Must Bring Jesus to a Humanity in Crisis," *Vatican Radio*, May 19, 2013.

16. Rose of Lima, *Ad Medicum Castillo*, ed. L. Getino (Madrid: La Patrona de America, 1928).

17. Adapted from *Bringing Christ to My Everyday World* by John J. Boucher (Locust Grove, VA: Chariscenter USA, 1990–1997), 2.

18. Synod of Bishops, *The New Evangelization for the Transmission of the Christian Faith: Lineamenta*, 2012, 12.

19. Charles Dollen, *Prayer Book of the Saints* (Huntington, IN: Our Sunday Visitor, 1984), 166.

20. John Paul II, *Novo Millennio Ineunte* [At the Beginning of the New Millennium], 2001, 40.

21. Some material adapted from "Why Don't Catholics Share Their Faith?" by Martin W. Pable, OFM, Cap, *America*, September 19, 2005. Reprinted with permission of America Press, Inc., © 2005. All rights reserved. For subscription information, call 1–800–627–9533 or visit www.americamagazine.org.

22. Therese Boucher, *A Prayer Journal for Baptism in the Holy Spirit* (Locust Grove, VA: National Service Committee, 2002), 7.

23. "St. Joseph Moscati," *Catholic News Agency*, November 16, 2013, http://www.catholicnewsagency.com/saint.php?n=55.

24. Committee on Evangelization and Catechesis, *Disciples Called to Witness: The New Evangelization* (Washington, DC: United States Conference of Catholic Bishops Inc., 2012), Part IV.

25. Chiffolo, 157.

26. "Benedict XVI Promotes Biblical Meditation," *ZENIT*, September 16, 2005, www.zenit.org/en/articles/benedict-xvi -promotes-biblical-meditation. Used by permission.

27. Dorothy Day, "Reflections During Advent, Part Four, Obedience," *Ave Maria*, December 17, 1966, 20–23, http:// www.catholicworker.org/dorothyday/Reprint2.cfm?TextID=562.

28. Adapted from *Evangelization Teams in the Making: A Catholic Parish Manual* by Dorothy Hulbert and Sr. Priscilla Lemire, RJM (Boca Raton, FL: Jeremiah Press, Inc. and NCCE, 2000), 14. Used by permission.

29. Schyler Rhodes, Stan Purdum, David J. Kalas, and Timothy J. Smith, *Sermons on the First Readings* (Lima, OH: CSS Publishing Company, Inc., 2007), 107.

30. Woodene Koenig-Bricker, *Praying with the Saints* (Chicago: Loyola Press, 2001), 162.

31. The Dominican Sisters of Hawthorne, "Rose Hawthorne, Candidate for Sainthood," *The Concord (MA) Magazine,* Autumn 2005, http://www.concordma.com/magazine/autumn05/rosehawthorne.html.

32. Fr. Tony Krisak, "Conversations About Faith," *Evangelization Exchange,* October 2010, http://www.pemdc.org/ee1010-conversations/.

33. Sherry Weddell, *Forming Intentional Disciples: The Path to Knowing and Following Jesus* (Huntington, IN: Our Sunday Visitor, 2012), 191–199.

34. Material adapted from *Heart to Heart Evangelization: Building Bridges Between Proclamation and Justice* by Susan Blum Gerding (Boca Raton, FL: Jeremiah Press, 1996), 16–17. Used by permission.

35. Diocese of Metuchen, "Prayer for the New Evangelization, 2012, http://diometuchen.org/offices-and-ministries/formation-and-leadership/evangelization/the-new-evangelization/.

36. Chiffolo, 123.

37. Fr. Tony Krisak, "Longing for an Invitation," *Evangelization Exchange*, May 2011, www.pemdc.org/ee0511-krisak/.

38. John Paul II, *Ecclesia in America* [The Church in America], January 22, 1999, 68.

39. John and Therese Boucher, *Keys for Welcoming Catholics Back to the Lord's Table* (Washington, DC: United Conference of Catholic Bishops, 2012), http://www.usccb.org/beliefs -and-teachings/how-we-teach/catechesis/catechetical-sunday/ new-evangelization/upload/keys-for-welcoming-boucher.pdf.

40. Dollen, 79.

41. "Bergoglio's Intervention: A Diagnosis of the Problems in the Church," *Vatican Radio,* March 27, 2013.

42. Josemaría Escríva, *Christ Is Passing By* (New Rochelle, NY: Scepter Publishers, 1974), 130.

43. For a more comprehensive treatment of meetings, please see www.christkey.com/parishmeetings.html.

44. Benedict XVI, "To the German Bishops," *L'Osservatore Romano*, Spanish Edition, August 26, 2005.

45. John Paul II, "Message of Pope John Paul II to the Youth on the Occasion of the 20th World Youth Day," August 6, 2005, 7.

46. Bert Ghezzi, *Voices of the Saints* (Chicago: Loyola Press, 2009), 187.

47. Benedict XVI, "Address to the Participants of the International Conference on the Occasion of the 40th Anniversary of the Conciliar Decree *Ad Gentes*," March 11, 2006.

48. Francis, "Address on the Vigil of Pentecost with the Ecclesial Movements," May 18, 2013.

49. Sr. Giacinta Basile, MPF, and Sr. Geraldine Calabrese, MPF, *Journeying with Lucy* (Morristown, NJ: Religious Teachers Filippini, 2001), 70.

50. United States Conference of Catholic Bishops, "Prayer for the New Evangelization," 2012, http://www.usccb.org/prayer-and -worship/prayers/new-evangelization-prayer.cfm.

51. Francis, "Homily, Sixth Sunday of Easter," May 5, 2013.

52. Barna Research Group, "Survey Shows How Christians Share Their Faith," Barna Research Group, January 31, 2005, https:// www.barna.org/barna-update/5-barna-update/186-survey -shows-how-christians-share-their-faith#.UkjWpNJ6bJY.

53. Some material adapted from "Fishing with Nets, Fishing with Poles: Reaching Inactive and Alienated Catholics," by Lorene Hanley Duquin, Paulist National Catholic Evangelization Association's Catholic Speakers Online Presentation, June 5, 2008, Adobe Flash file, 58:17, http://www.pemdc.org/events/cso -duquin.aspx. Used by permission.

54. John Paul II, "Internet: A New Forum for Proclaiming the Gospel," Message for the 36th World Communications Day, May 12, 2002.

55. For more information on this topic, please go to http://www .renewalministries.net/files/freeliterature/Charisms%20OSV_ June%2013_07.pdf.

56. Albert L. Winseman, "How Many Americans Are 'Unchurched'?" Gallup, Inc., October 11, 2005, http://www .gallup.com/poll/19129/how-many-americans-unchurched.aspx.